VICTORY in SURRENDER

Captivating Stories and Testimonies

Dr. Susan Mbaluka

Victory in Surrender

Dr. Susan Mbaluka

Hope Publishers
Houston, Texas

Published in the United States by Hope Publishers
Houston Texas
Email: hopepublisherss@yahoo.com

Layout by Hope Publishers
All photos credited to Hope Publishers.

Printed in the United States of America

ACKNOWLEDGEMENTS

My highest honor goes to God before I acknowledge the invaluable contribution of various people who helped me accomplish this project. God provided the aspiration, wisdom, knowledge, life itself, and all the necessary resources to write a book like this. Next, some people walked with me through the entire journey of this book's authorship—the Mbalukas: David, Wisdom, and Beatrice. They encouraged me to keep on writing until it was done. Wisdom was the first to read the manuscript and to provide feedback. He was both my supporter and reviewer. Later, Beatrice read the document and provided invaluable feedback. David encouraged me to write even when it seemed hard. Thanks to my family for understanding when I focused on writing for hours.

Thanks to Pastor Christopher Mwashinga for his continuous encouragement. Having authored more than a dozen books himself, he gave me crucial guidance. On completing the manuscript, Mwashinga read it, offered constructive feedback, and later guided me through the publishing process. Thank you, brother.

Dr. Ashwin Somasundram, as my pastor of ten years, contributed to this book in many ways. Thank you for allowing God to use you to mentor me spiritually. You read *Victory in Surrender* and provided vital feedback. May God bless you indeed.

An exceptional thanks to Dr. Bordes Henry Saturné, who read the manuscript and gave me feedback that prompted me to add the subtitle of this book. Pastor Zablon Zcube reviewed the manuscript, and his experience in writing his own books was evident in his feedback. I am grateful to you, man of God.

Many thanks go to my friends and church family. They offered many prayers for the completion of this book, and received my first book with excitement. Their response was encouraging. Thanks to them all.

TABLE OF CONTENTS

ACKNOWLEDGEMENTS 5

FOREWORD 9

INTRODUCTION 13

Chapter 1 Total Surrender 15

Chapter 2 The Enemy of Surrender 22

Chapter 3 Unbelief: The Hindrance 30

Chapter 4 Fear That Thwarts Surrender 38

Chapter 5 Blessings for the Surrendered 46

Chapter 6 The Time Factor 54

Chapter 7 Allowing God's Will to Be Done in You 60

Chapter 8 Transformation 66

Chapter 9 A Peculiar Life 72

Chapter 10 Obedience in Surrender 78

Chapter 11 Trusting God With Your Life 82

Chapter 12 Leaning on God 88

Chapter 13 Heeding the Commission 93

Chapter 14 Influencing Others for Christ 101

Chapter 15 God Prepares His Workers 105

Chapter 16 Your Service to God 114

Chapter 17 The Lord's Battle 118

Chapter 18 Victory Is Assured 123

Chapter 19 Choice and Destiny 129

Chapter 20 Getting Ready for the Kingdom 138

ENDNOTES 143

FOREWORD

Life-changing books are written by changed lives. These books are so powerful because the authors have been shaken to their core, and their experience shakes us. We are moved because they have been moved, and we are transformed because they have been transformed. I have witnessed how Dr. Susan Mbaluka's life has been radically changed by the truths she shares in *Victory in Surrender*. For the past 10 years in my capacity as her Pastor, mentor, friend, and co-laborer in God's kingdom, I have observed, firsthand, that she is the personification of life totally surrendered to God. Whether it be through her work as a gifted Christian educator, diligent church administrator, or passionate church ministry leader, Susan makes our invisible God visible!

In her timely book, Dr. Mbaluka's message to the readers is that the surprising key to unlocking their potential and experiencing the sense of peace and purpose they crave is nothing less than total surrender to God. She posits, "Total surrender to God is the essence of Christianity." There is a gnawing inside all of us that tells us we can be better. If we could just get a break or be more organized or work a little harder, we could break free from the struggles we face and become the persons we know we were intended to be. But what is the message of the cross? It is not God saying, "I died for your sins, and now I will work as a consultant in your life to help you achieve the life you are determined to have." No! Jesus died as a model for us to die and give our lives to God and others—the total surrender to God is indeed a tremendous spiritual victory.

Dr. Mbaluka's core message is that if our hearts are willing to surrender everything into God's hands, there is no end to what He will do for us—no end to the blessings He will bestow. Her wise counsel will enable you to take a giant step closer to God as you begin your journey into perfect peace and trust. We cannot always determine the circumstances in our lives, but perspective and peace amid the stormy chaos of life are always available to the person who wins the battle to live a surrendered life. It is possible to have a life filled with meaning, purpose, and joy. *Victory in surrender* contains the promise of a pathway to wholeness, fulfillment, and peace with God.

I highly recommend this book to anyone interested in experiencing the transformative power of the gospel. It is life-changing, genuine, and challenging. Thank you, Dr. Mbaluka, for taking us closer to the heart of God.

Dr. Ashwin Somasundram, Senior Pastor, West Houston SDA Church

Amidst the deluge of 21st-century information, one may feel lost in a forest, seeking a meaningful way out. The search for a pathway out of the forest requires a careful identification of the compass directions and a decision on which direction to pursue for a desired end. There are some who feel lost in the forest of life and attempt their way out by trial and error, groping in darkness as it were, trying to reach a direction they do not know. And yet life, as we have it in this world, has an end. Any time lost cannot be regained. Hence, trial and error is not the best way to pursue a critical destiny in life. Fortunately, we can learn from others how to successfully navigate the forest.

Victory in Surrender is a powerful guide and encouragement for a meaningful life journey. Some of the great lessons in life come packaged in what may appear to be contradictory. *Victory in*

Surrender is one such inspiring package. It is a testimony, an experience of one whose life has been transformed in a significant way and is happy to share the testimony passionately, accompanied by life stories that will capture the reader's attention and illustrate the power of surrender in gaining victory.

In reading through this book, the author, Dr. Susan Mbaluka, led me to reflect on my own spiritual journey. I was made to confront my fears and worries of life to embrace the wonderful blessings that come with surrender. Indeed God works best and more effectively with those who have learned to surrender. He lifts such to greater spiritual heights that only God can do. As a result of this relationship with God, a new life ensures which is evidenced by a passionate desire and willingness to obey and trust God unreservedly. Being so equipped, you are led to face battles of life, realizing one victory after another regardless of the fierceness of the battles you may encounter.

In this transformation journey, Dr. Mbaluka shares, using real-life illustrations, how your life gets transformed when you are engaged in service to God and humankind. Such a transformed life results in a life of service, and it is here that you will experience full joy and find true purpose and meaning in life.

To you, the reader, I say, have an exciting journey reading *Victory in Surrender: Captivating Stories and Testimonies*. Like Abraham, God is saying to you, "Go from your country, your people, and your father's household to the land I will show you." Genesis 12:1 (NIV). Jesus Christ will go with you, and God, the Father, is waiting anxiously to receive you on the other side. God bless you as you take the journey.

Geoffrey G. Mbwana, General Vice President, General Conference of Seventh-day Adventists

Many times, Christianity appears as a category in which people fit based on their families' religious traditions rather than the identity of a person in a personal relationship with Jesus. This book highlights what it takes to live an authentic Christian life. Dr. Susan Mbaluka says, "Faith in Jesus does not only redeem from sin but also restores people to the image of God." Further, Dr. Mbaluka poses the vital question of all times: "Can people live sinless lives on earth? Or is it enough to be active church members?" These concepts are clearly and interestingly elaborated. The message in this book is essential and timely.

Pastor Stephen Paul Muasya, General Field Secretary, East-Central Africa Division of Seventh-day Adventist

INTRODUCTION

When I first got the idea of writing a book on victory in surrender, I took a few minutes to think about the juxtaposition in the title. Usually, people do not triumph through submission. Typically, to be called a fighter is a compliment. But Scripture makes it clear that God gives us victory by surrendering to the Lord, Jesus Christ (Luke 17:33).

Total surrender to God is the essence of Christianity. Going to church or becoming a church member does not indicate conversion. The impression of writing a book on victory through surrender fascinated me after I came to the realization that identifying with religion or attending church does not equal a relationship with Christ.

The principle of total surrender to God involves a matter of life and death that every person, who wants eternal life, should consider solemnly. Hence, this book presents serious life matters that I learned through prayer, a diligent search of Scripture, Bible commentaries, religious writings, and consultations with pastors who are seasoned authors of religious works and scholars of the Word of God. The content calls attention to what surrender to the Lord entails, the enemies of surrender, and how to overcome each one of them to establish and retain a loving relationship with Christ.

It is my sincere prayer that this book will propel you to the most powerful Christian experience, and a personal and intimate relationship with God, which leads to incredible victory over evil. A close relationship with the Lord will keep you changing into His image as you wait for Him to take you home.

As you read one chapter to the next, expect interesting stories and testimonies that explain the concepts and plenty of examples of people who surrendered fully to God and the outcome of their surrender. I encourage you to look up the Bible verses and other quotes that I cite in the text.

I pray that the purpose of this book—to exhort and assist you to surrender yourself totally to God and to enter into a loving relationship with Him—will be realized in you. Keep reading to the end as you pray for the grace to surrender yourself fully to God.

Chapter 1

Total Surrender

"My feet need rest from the emergency brakes," said a passenger.

"You have no brake pedal under your feet. How are you applying the brakes?" asked the driver. "I've been pressing on imaginary brakes to slow down the car," the passenger said. The driver got the message: He needed to slow down to the speed limit.

Have you ever tried to apply emergency brakes in a vehicle in which you were a passenger, with no brake pedal under your feet? I have. That happens especially when a person is uncomfortable with the speed or the driving style of the driver.

Who is in the driver's seat of your life? Is it God or someone else? Do you trust the driving skills of your driver? Whoever is in the driver's seat is in control of your life. And if God is in control of your life, you can rest assured that you are safe. But if someone else is in charge of your life, you are not safe. "Trust in the Lord with all your heart, and lean not on your own understanding; in all your ways acknowledge Him, and He shall direct your paths" (Proverbs 3:5, 6).

When sin entered into the lives of Adam and Eve, it separated them and their offspring from God (Isaiah 59:2). It destroyed humans in every sense, including their thinking capacity, the power to live godly lives, and even the functioning of their physical bodies. Thus, instead of humans becoming like God—as Satan had told Eve—the image of God in them was greatly destroyed. Sin put humanity in Satan's grasp. For that reason, Christ died to set us free and to restore us to the image of God. The Savior paved the way for us to go back to God's leadership and total restoration of our relationship with Him. For Christ to save us and reconcile us with God, we must accept Him as our Savior and the Lord of our lives. Thus, we must accept His redemption and cooperate with Him to empower us to overcome evil daily.

Let me explain this reality with a story from my childhood. When I was growing up, young people had a way of submitting themselves to stronger peers who could fight bullies on their behalf, especially on their way home from school. Up to the early 1980s, there were very few schools, especially in most rural parts of Kenya. Most children had to walk long distances to and from school. I was one of those whose home was far from school, and as we trekked the long distances of dusty earth roads through the woods, bullies picked on those they deemed weak to instigate fights. But there was a solution to the problem.

If you, the one bullied, wanted to avoid pain, all you needed to do was to run to a friend much bigger and stronger than the bully and ask him or her to fight on your behalf. Then your surrogate would say, “If you want me to fight for you, hold your forehead.” As soon as your hand touched your forehead, the surrogate blows would rain on the bully until he or she ran for dear life.

Jesus is our only solution for sin and all the problems it causes in our lives. But even though God’s love for us is immeasurable, He does not save us or take charge of our lives by force. We need to let Him willingly. To accept Jesus Christ as the Savior and Lord of our lives is to allow God to come into our lives, who, in turn, forgives our sins and starts restoring us to our original state, changing us from sinful beings back to godly people. But if we reject Jesus Christ, we allow Satan to continue holding us and influencing our minds and hearts to sin. So we either have God or Satan working in our lives; there is no middle ground in spiritual matters.

A person may say, "I am a baptized church member. I have a powerful ministry, and I always contribute to help the church." But have you surrendered your life totally to God? Do you allow God to change your mind and your heart to reflect His image? Is Jesus the Lord of your life?

It is one thing to say we are Christians and attend church every week. It is another thing to let God change and empower us so much that we reflect His image in every aspect of our lives. When we surrender fully to God, we manifest the fruit of the Holy Spirit: love for God and humankind, "joy, peace, longsuffering, kindness, goodness, faithfulness, gentleness, and self-control" (Galatians 5:22, 23). The character of God is seen in every true Christian.

In *Ministry of Healing*, Ellen. G. White explains surrender very well. She says, "The mere hearing of sermons…the reading of the Bible through and through, or the explanation of it verse by verse, will not benefit us or those who hear us unless we bring the truths of the Bible into our individual experience. The understanding, the will, the affections, must be yielded to the control of the word of God. Then through the work of the Holy Spirit, the precepts of the word will become the principles of the life."[1] We cannot overemphasize the importance of realizing that Jesus did not only die to redeem us but also to restore us to the image of God, the character of God, which we had before sin came into the world. Therefore, after we accept Jesus as our Savior, we also need to allow Him to be the Lord of our lives. We need to obey His Word. Thus, God wants us to open ourselves to Him without any reservations. When we do, He comes into our lives and gradually changes us. Then we get empowered to live our lives according to biblical principles. That calls for total surrender and commitment to God.

Commitment is very crucial in every activity that a person undertakes. People admire whenever they see it in a person's life, especially through a worthy cause. Nelson Mandela, former president of South Africa, is an example of someone who is highly esteemed for his commitment to fighting apartheid in South Africa. He sacrificed his life for the freedom of his country. It is amazing how Mandela spent 27 years of his life in prison instead of giving in to apartheid. Even after spending those decades in jail, he still insisted on the eradication of discrimination based on race at the time of his release. In other words, Mandela was willing to die in prison if that was what it took to end apartheid.[2] How more deeply should we commit ourselves to God for eternal life?

The Role of the Holy Spirit in Surrender

The Holy Spirit plays an essential role in surrender. It is the Holy Spirit who helps us to realize our un-surrendered, sinful condition, the danger of eternal death, and the need of a Savior (John 16:8). He entreats us to give our lives to God. If we yield and repent our sins, God forgives us. The blood of Jesus washes our sins away. Our faith in the Lord, Jesus Christ, makes it possible. Then the Holy Spirit works on the surrendered to continue growing into the image of God, all justified. "But you were washed, but you were sanctified, but you were justified in the name of the Lord Jesus and by the Spirit of our God" (1Corinthians 6:11).

God wants His people to be filled with the Holy Spirit, who is the source of power in the life of a surrendered Christian. "See then that you walk circumspectly, not as fools but as wise, redeeming the time, because the days are evil. Therefore, do not be unwise, but understand what the will of the Lord is… be filled with the Spirit" (Ephesians 5: 15-18). The Holy Spirit enables God's people to live new lives in Christ (Titus 3:5). He empowers the surrendered to overcome sin.

In one of Dr. Ashwin Somasundram's sermons, he said that since God instructs His people to be filled with the Holy Spirit, it is disobedience to the Lord not to be filled with the Spirit. Moreover, he gives a three-step process to receive the Holy Spirit. Step one is to yearn for a life pleasing to the Lord. "Blessed are those who hunger and thirst for righteousness, For they shall be filled" (Mathew 5:6). Step two, ask. "Ask and it will be given to you" (Mathew 7:7). God tells us to ask. Hence, we need to ask Him to forgive us, cleanse us from sin, and fill us with His Holy Spirit. Finally, step three is surrender. You must be willing to give your life a hundred percent to Jesus. For the Holy Spirit to fill us, we have to allow God to empty us of our "old self," as described in Ephesians 4:22. The "old self" refers to our un-converted condition. We need to allow God to cleanse us from all unrighteousness, such as pride, unbelief, selfishness, gossip, hatred, anger, unforgiveness, lust, and any other sin.

Every genuine Christian must be filled with the Holy Spirit. "Because the carnal mind is enmity against God; for it is not subject to the law of God, nor indeed can be. So then, those who are in the flesh cannot please God. But you are not in the flesh but in the Spirit, if indeed the Spirit of God dwells in you. Now if anyone does not have the Spirit of Christ, he is not His" (Romans 8:7-9). Let us all ask God to fill us with His Holy Spirit. If we are willing, the Lord will take care of the process and guide us throughout our lives.

Going all the Way

After his conversion, the apostle Paul lived an exemplary life of total surrender and commitment to God. He said, "I have been crucified with Christ; it is no longer I who live, but Christ lives in me; and the life which I now live in the flesh I live by faith in the Son of God, who loved me and gave Himself for me" (Galatians 2:20). Paul's old sinful nature had lost power over him as a result of Christ's victory in his life. As a converted person, Paul lived a surrendered life to Christ. Hence, he was able to achieve great success in his Christian life and service to God. We see great commitment and victory in his work of taking the gospel to the Gentiles. His numerous mission trips portray Paul as someone who was so dedicated to his calling that not even beatings or imprisonment could stop him.

Toward the end of his life, he said, "I have fought the good fight, I have finished the race, I have kept the faith. Finally, there is laid up for me the crown of righteousness, which the Lord, the righteous Judge, will give to me on that Day, and not to me only but also to all who have loved His appearing" (2 Timothy 4:7,8). What a sense of a life well-lived for God! What great self-actualization!

God calls us to surrender ourselves to Him and to be fully committed to our faith. "If anyone desires to come after Me, let him deny himself, and take up his cross, and follow Me. For whoever desires to save his life will lose it, but whoever loses his life for My sake will find it" (Matthew 16:24, 25). The emphasis of this Scripture is a call for total surrender to the Lord, Jesus Christ. First, one must reject or denounce anything contrary to Christian principles. The goal is to resemble the Master in every aspect of one's life. Second, the disciple must pick up his or her cross. That calls for a willingness to endure whatever suffering that will come along the way. Finally, the follower of Christ is called to follow in His footsteps, who selflessly focused on the good of others, feeding and teaching people about the Word of God.

Jesus is the perfect example of total surrender to God. He committed His life to achieve something of the highest value. The Lord left His paradise in heaven, came to earth to be born like us, and to experience our struggles and sufferings. Yet, He surrendered totally to the will of God.

Through the guidance of the Holy Spirit, the Word of God and prayer, we learn to let God lead us to surrender to Him fully, which is a process that starts from the time we accept Jesus Christ as our Savior. At that point, we get reconciled to God. “But as many as received Him, to them He gave the right to become children of God, to those who believe in His name” (John 1:12). The journey of surrender continues throughout life, which requires that we read the Word of God daily and pray for the Holy Spirit to dwell in us to teach and guide us. That is necessary to overcome the enemy of surrender as we wait for the Lord to take us home.

It does not matter how much we have sinned. It does not matter how many times we have failed. God's love for us is inexhaustible. All we need is to allow Him in our lives. Then He will change our hearts and minds and enable us to live victorious Christian lives. That is necessary to overcome the enemy and all the vices he uses to thwart our surrender to God. Will you let Christ work in you and enable you to overcome sin?

Chapter 2

The Enemy of Surrender

Satan is the archenemy of surrender to God (Ephesians 6:11–13). Pride and self-exaltation originated in Satan to such an extent that he sought to be equal with God. He said, "I will ascend above the heights of the clouds, I will be like the Most High" (Isaiah 14:14). Then Lucifer, the angel of light, with perfect beauty and intelligence, (Ezekiel28:12), became the devil, who opposes God. "And war broke out in heaven: Michael and his angels fought with the dragon; and the dragon and his angels fought, but they did not prevail, nor was a place found for them in heaven any longer. So the great dragon was cast out, that serpent of old, called the Devil and Satan, who deceives the whole world; he was cast to the earth, and his angels were cast out with him" (Revelation 12:7-9).

Since then, Satan became the archenemy of God, who stands between people and their surrender to God. The devil deceives people to rebel against God as he did. The workings of this cunning adversary are manifested through various vices, including pride, unbelief, and fear. In this chapter, we will focus on pride, which is discussed in two components: self-sufficiency and arrogance. Once this vice is allowed to thrive in people's hearts, it impedes surrender to God; it destroys people's relationship with Him and fellow human beings. I concur with C.S. Lewis that "pride is spiritual cancer: it eats up the very possibility of love, or contentment, or even common sense."[1] The Bible has much to say about pride, as we will see in the following pages.

Self-sufficiency

In this chapter, self-sufficiency refers to an attitude of independence from God, meaning that the people who maintain that attitude believe that they have no need for God in their lives. The *King James Bible Dictionary* defines self-sufficiency as "excessive confidence in one's own competence or sufficiency."[2] Genesis chapter 1 tells us that God created everything that was made. And He is the sustainer of life. Therefore, disregarding God in one's life is a way of portraying pride. And that is a prevailing attitude in the world today. When people believe that they do not need God in their lives, they shut the door to the Holy Spirit, who teaches and leads them to the Savior. That is one major characteristic of proud people. They resist God. Yet, Scripture says, "Everyone proud in the heart is an abomination to the Lord" (Proverbs 16:5). Pride desecrates a person.

Regardless of the reasons that people have for shutting God out of their lives, nothing in the world can satisfy the soul like God. Every good thing that we get is by the grace of God. Let me tell you about a situation that reminded me of this lesson very well. In 2010, a few months after I moved from Tennessee to Houston, Texas, I became sick and fatigued. I tried to maintain a positive attitude as I worked on a curriculum that I was developing at the time. But it reached a point where I could not do much. Cooking lunch for my family drained me for the rest of the day. The work that I usually finished in three weeks took me a much longer time.

I wondered *I have always done whatever I set my mind to do and have met deadlines. I thought I was very industrious and highly focused. What has happened to me?* I never imagined a situation where I could not produce the desired results in whatever activity I set my mind. Then I realized that whenever I attained anything, God made it possible for me to achieve it by giving me good health, peace of mind, finances, and a conducive environment in which to work, whether on my education or other projects. Deuteronomy 8 had never been more meaningful to me:

> Beware that you do not forget the LORD your God by not keeping His commandments, His judgments, and His statutes which I command you today, lest—*when* you have eaten and are full, and have built beautiful houses and dwell *in them;* and *when* your herds and your flocks multiply, and your silver and your gold are multiplied, and all that you have is multiplied; when your heart is lifted up, and you forget the LORD your God who brought you out of the land of Egypt, from the house of bondage…And you shall remember the LORD your God, for it is He who gives you power to get wealth, that He may establish His covenant which He swore to your fathers, as it is this day. (Deut. 8:11-14, 18)

This message is as relevant to us today as it was to the Israelites when they prepared to enter the Promised Land. We all have our bondage from which the Lord liberated us through His son, Jesus Christ. The Lord provides for all our needs. With much love, God tells us to be careful not to fall into the unfortunate situation of taking His blessings for granted, or worse, drifting away and eventually rejecting Him as a result of our success. However, rejecting God, openly, is not the only portrayal of self-sufficiency; people may attend church regularly and still be guilty of it.

Many join churches, but all they have is a religion without any personal relationship with the Lord. They go to God with their righteousness, which they believe is good enough to earn them salvation. They neither have regard for God's will nor guidance from His Word. That is self-sufficiency, which stems from pride. In the parable of the Pharisee and the tax collector, Jesus warned people about this attitude (Luke 18:12-14).

The Pharisee had religion, but he was too proud to submit to God. He believed that his actions were sufficient to earn him salvation. He felt no need to confess his sins or to seek God's guidance and power to live a holy life. Sadly, that attitude did not end with the Pharisee, and it prevents people from yielding to God's Holy Spirit. Human righteousness is stained by sin (Isaiah 64:6). For that reason, it cannot earn anybody's salvation.

One of my former colleagues told me an interesting statement about the peacock. She said that the peacock believes that it is so beautiful because of its feathers. But it never looks at its feet to realize that they are not as beautiful as the feathers. Similarly, the Kamba people, one of the tribes in Kenya, have a saying that whoever evaluates oneself sees no faults (Mwilungi ndeiluu). Have you ever caught yourself with the peacock's attitude? I have. And the Holy Spirit has remarkably interesting ways of leading me out of those situations.

In the story of the Pharisee and the tax collector, Jesus praised the humility of the tax collector, who recognized his need for God's forgiveness and mercy. "And the tax collector, standing afar off, would not so much as raise his eyes to heaven, but beat his breast, saying, 'God, be merciful to me a sinner!' I tell you, this man went down to his house justified rather than the other; for everyone who exalts himself will be humbled, and he who humbles himself will be exalted" (Luke 18:13, 14). It is a blessing to recognize the need for God in our lives and to give our lives entirely to Him. It is equally important to realize the need for us to depend on God for our salvation because our efforts will not get us anywhere near heaven.

In *The Desire of Ages,* White notes, "The proud heart strives to earn salvation, but both our title to heaven and our fitness for it are found in the righteousness of Christ. The Lord can do nothing toward the recovery of man until convinced of his own weakness, and stripped of all self-sufficiency, he yields himself to the control of God."[3] Thus, self-sufficiency prevents people from allowing Christ to cleanse them from their sins and to empower them to live victorious, Christian lives. Arrogance is another component of pride that Satan uses to thwart people's surrender to God.

Arrogance

According to the *Cambridge Dictionary*, arrogance is being "proud in an unpleasant way and behaving as if you are better or more important than other people."[4] Arrogant people are among the wicked that the Bible warns so strongly about: "Slanderers, God-haters, insolent, arrogant and boastful; they invent ways of doing evil; they disobey their parents; they have no understanding, no fidelity, no love, no mercy. Although they know God's righteous decree that those who do such things deserve death, they not only continue to do these very things but also approve of those who practice them" (Romans 1:30–32, NIV). Sadly, the arrogant are in the same category as God-haters. The boastful manifest arrogance in many ways, including bragging. The last part of the verse says that the arrogant know that God's judgment will fall on those who do such things, but they do them, nonetheless. Also, they endorse similar behavior in others.

You may have heard someone say, "I'm not arrogant; I just can't stand some people." Or "I'm not proud; I just can't bend that low." Is it bending too low to say sorry when you wrong another person? Is it bending too low to talk to a brother or sister lovingly to correct them when they are wrong? Even in professed Christians, pride shows its ugly face sometimes. Many times, we get into bad relationships with our relatives, workmates, or even neighbors, all because of pride. If I think I am better than my sister, brother, neighbor, or colleague, that attitude will show in my choice of words, tone, body language, and actions. When these attitudes are taken a step further, we treat those we belittle as if they have no human feelings, as if they never get humiliated or embarrassed. Arrogance makes people so insensitive that they demonstrate a lack of compassion for others who need empathy the most. Yet many life experiences show how wrong a proud attitude can be.

A few years ago, students, teachers, and staff at my school played a game that demonstrated the need for God and other people in our lives. On that day, we took students to a forest in Cleveland, Tennessee, and placed them into groups of six. One teacher or staff member joined each group, making it seven people per group.

Then we tied a long, strong, but thin chain between two trees. Each group was supposed to get one of their members to walk on the chain. To do so, one needed the support of the group members. The person who volunteered to walk for the group stood on the chain using the shoulders of the group members as support. As the volunteer walked on the chain, the group members provided support to the end. Thus, all the group members depended on the two trees to which the chain was tied. The group won the top prize if the person walked from one end of the string to the other without falling.

After all the groups had participated, we assembled in one place. Then the group manager told us, "The trees on which we tied the chain represent God, who is the strongest and most dependable of all. Just as we all needed the trees, we all need God in our lives. Also, the group represented all the people that we interact with in life—family, friends, schoolmates, neighbors, workmates, or even strangers. Just as the volunteer needed the support of the group, we all need each other as we go through life. Thus, we need God, and we also need each other." That was a moment of serious thinking and reflecting for me as I offered a silent prayer for victory over pride.

Bible verses such as Romans 12:16 came to mind, "Live in harmony with one another. Do not be proud, but be willing to associate with people of low position. Do not be conceited" (NIV), and "The sacrifices of God are a broken spirit, A broken and contrite heart-These, O God, You will not despise" (Psalm 51:17).

Pride is very offensive to God. It hinders people from realizing their need for the Savior. Pride takes the place of a "broken, contrite heart," and there is no remorse for sin. Instead of humbly repenting their sins, proud people stubbornly insist on their ways, even when they know that they are contrary to God's will. They may also make excuses, for they find fault with everyone but themselves. C.S. Lewis sums it well in his quote, "As long as you are proud, you cannot know God. A proud man is always looking down on things and people: and, of course, as long as you are looking down, you cannot see something that is above you."[5]

God calls on His people to humble themselves. True humility enables people to see themselves for who they are: sinners in need of a Savior. And it shows itself when we are dealing with people who are in a lesser position than us, in terms of education, power, wealth, or physical disability. John Dickson rightly defines humility as "the noble choice to forgo your status, deploy your resources, or use your influence for the good of others before yourself." He further says that humility is a "virtue with aesthetics, logic, and practical benefits."[6] Humility is beautiful when you see it, and like any other spiritual victory, it comes through God's grace.

When we surrender ourselves to God, He handles pride for us and gives us the grace to love and to honor Him in our lives. He enables us to love and to treat others with respect. Once we give ourselves totally to God, we do not need to worry about self-sufficiency, arrogance, or any other sin that the devil uses to destroy our relationship with God. The Lord replaces our pride with humility and love. He reveals Himself to us more and more. Then we can hear the voice of the Holy Spirit, leading us in our lives. Will you surrender fully to God and let Him give you the grace to humble yourself to Him? Next, we will explore the seriousness of unbelief concerning surrender.

Chapter 3

Unbelief: The Hindrance

The *King James Version Bible Dictionary* defines unbelief as "the withholding of belief or disbelief of the truth of the gospel."[1] That involves distrusting God and not accepting that Jesus Christ is the Savior. No wonder unbelief hinders surrender and any genuine relationship with God. Let me tell you about a time when I experienced difficulties believing information that was supposed to be taken very seriously by all it concerned.

In mid-August 2017, both local and national television channels, social media, and radios warned about a deadly hurricane, tornados, and floods that would hit Texas. Hurricane Harvey was forecast to hit the south of Texas, from August 25 to 29. Unprecedented rainfall and flooding were expected in many parts, especially in the city of Houston. People who lived on the South Coast around Corpus Christi, where the hurricane was to strike, received mandatory evacuation orders. Others, whose homes were near rivers, dams, and bayous, were told to expect terrible flooding. They, too, were advised to move to safer places.

As a then-resident of Houston, I paid keen attention to the warnings. A week before the hurricane hit, every news outlet bombarded us with notifications—even those who did not need to evacuate their homes required to prepare for the terrible catastrophe. For instance, we knew that we could experience blackouts, so we needed to have some form of alternative lighting. At first, I thought to myself: *we have experienced many tornadoes and floods before. Do people have to leave their homes to go to a shelter, even before the rain starts? Maybe it will not be as bad as it sounds.*

But the warnings were very persistent. For the first time in my life, our church secretary sent out an email and canceled church service that weekend. Most people who lived in areas that were deemed dangerous, evacuated—fortunately, my neighborhood was not one of them. While many people heeded the warnings and moved from their homes beforehand, some did not.

Unfortunately, the hurricane struck. I had never witnessed such heavy rain in my life. Houses, buildings, roads, and fields flooded. Most of those who ignored the evacuation warnings called for help after their homes or apartments received several feet of floodwater. The torrents swept cars down to the ocean. Tornadoes flattened homes, while property worth millions of dollars got destroyed by water in homes or businesses. Worse yet, lives were lost. Then it dawned on me that the warnings deserved the urgency with which they were given.

At the same time, I witnessed incredible kindness from people from all over the United States. People came from other states and cities to Houston to help. Some volunteers came with their boats to ferry people who were stuck in their flooded homes while others came to work in shelters or distribution centers. Others helped to clean the flooded buildings. But the majority of people who did not personally come to Texas sent all kinds of donations, food, clothing, or money.

As I watched these acts of love and kindness, my mind switched to a more serious event that is sure to happen to the planet earth. I wondered how many people know or believe that Jesus will come back to take His people home and that this world will come to an end. Suppose those who believe in God and have surrendered themselves to Christ went out of their way to encourage others to give their lives to Christ before it is too late! Suppose every Christian acted with the sense of urgency that I witnessed during Hurricane Harvey! How many would believe the gospel of Jesus Christ?

Then I remembered Noah's story. God instructed him to build an ark to take in people and animals to save them from a deadly flood that was going to cover the whole earth. But after Noah preached for 120 years, only his family of eight believed him and entered the ark. It was not until the rains poured, and the floods started covering everything that people ran to the ark to ask Noah to open the door and let them in. But it was too late. They perished in the floods, all because they wouldn't believe God's warning through Noah. How sad! Without surrender to the Lord, the danger of unbelief is still a threat to us today.

Examples of Unbelief

We already saw that unbelief involves distrusting God and not accepting that Jesus Christ is the Savior. Hebrews 3:12 tells us that unbelief is evil, and it manifests itself in moving away from God. We see many instances when the children of Israel portrayed unbelief. Examples include their murmurings in the wilderness, recorded in the Old Testament, and later the refusal of the Jewish leaders to believe that Jesus Christ was the Savior, as we read in the New Testament. They saw the works that Jesus performed and listened to His teachings, but while many others believed in Him, the leaders decided to get rid of Him. The following quote, which was a conversation between the Jewish leaders and some officers whom the leaders had sent to arrest Jesus, portray the leaders' determination not to believe in the Lord:

> Then the officers came to the chief priests and Pharisees, who said to them, "Why have you not brought Him?"
>
> The officers answered, "No man ever spoke like this Man!"
>
> Then the Pharisees answered them, "Are you also deceived? Have any of the rulers or the Pharisees believed in Him? But this crowd that does not know the law is accursed." (John 7:45- 49)

The preceding conversation shows that the rulers and the Pharisees had every reason to believe in Jesus. The wisdom and power with which Jesus taught were so convincing to those who heard Him. But the leaders of the people demeaned those who believed in Him. The crucifixion of Jesus, and later the killings of the apostles, were acts of unbelief. The words of Stephen to the people of Israel tell us more of what happens when unbelief enfolds. He said to them, "You stiff-necked and uncircumcised in heart and ears! You always resist the Holy Spirit; as your fathers did, so do you" (Acts 7:51). Unbelief prevents people from yielding to the Holy Spirit of God.

In *The Great Controversy*, Ellen White describes unbelief very well. She says, "Distrust of God is the natural outgrowth of the unrenewed heart, which is at enmity with Him. But faith is inspired by the Holy Spirit, and it will flourish only as it is cherished... Unbelief strengthens as it is encouraged."[2]

I believe that the story about the 12 spies whom Moses sent to cross over to the Promised Land to spy and take back a report to Moses and the children of Israel is another clear example of unbelief. The men sent as spies were the heads of the houses of Israel. They had seen God's mercy and His power in leading and providing for the Israelites. But the report 10 of the 12 spies took back was one of despair and unbelief. They said,

"We can't attack those people; they are stronger than we are." And they spread among the Israelites a bad report about the land they had explored. They said, "The land we explored devours those living in it. All the people we saw there are of great size." (Numbers 13:31-32 NIV)

So all the congregation lifted up their voices and cried, and the people wept that night. And all the children of Israel complained against Moses and Aaron, and the whole congregation said to them, "If only we had died in the land of Egypt! Or if only we had died in this wilderness! Why has the LORD brought us to this land to fall by the sword, that our wives and children should become victims? Would it not be better for us to return to Egypt?" So they said to one another, "Let us select a leader and return to Egypt." (Numbers 14: 1-4)

As far as human power was concerned, the Israelites were unable to conquer the inhabitants of Canaan. But up to that point, it had only been God's power that sustained them. It was not easy to part the Red Sea for the Israelites to walk on dry land. Neither was it any easier to cause water to flow from a rock or to rain manna to feed the Israelites. God was leading them, and just as He had overcome the Egyptians and other obstacles along the way, He was able to get the land of Canaan for them, as He had promised.

But the people kept on distrusting God and opposing Him. They did not believe God, no matter what He did for them. They did not trust in His promises. For that reason, they murmured against Moses, Aaron, and God. They even went as far as choosing a leader to take them back to Egypt. That was unbelief in the deepest sense of the word. So, their self-fulfilling prophecy came to pass. They told themselves that they were not able to defeat the inhabitants of Canaan, so God allowed it to happen just as they had said. As a result, for 40 years they wandered in the wilderness until the entire older generation died. As Christians, do we ever prophesy doom on ourselves instead of claiming God's promises by faith?

While the ten spies and the congregation of the Israelites doubted the power and the faithfulness of God to give them the Promised Land, Joshua and Caleb believed that God was able to overcome the giants and settle the Israelites in Canaan. The two men tore their clothes, for it grieved them that the people of God did not believe in Him. Hence, Joshua and Caleb spoke to the Israelites, describing the land as incredibly good. They said because the Lord is faithful, He would honor His promise to them. Caleb and Joshua pleaded with the people not to rebel against God. They encouraged them not to fear the inhabitants of Canaan. Remember, Joshua and Caleb were among the 12 who spied on the land of Canaan. The two faithful men saw the same land, the same huge people that the other spies saw, and all twelve men had witnessed God's power throughout their journey from Egypt to that point. What made the difference? How come they came up with a different report from the rest? Unbelief in the ten spies versus faith and trust in the hearts of Joshua and Caleb made all the difference. As White states,

> Those who desire to doubt will have plenty of room. God does not propose to remove all occasion for unbelief. He gives evidence, which must be carefully investigated with a humble mind and a teachable spirit, and all should decide from the weight of evidence. God gives sufficient evidence for the candid mind to believe; but he who turns from the weight of the evidence because there are a few things which he cannot make plain to his finite understanding will be left in the cold, chilling atmosphere of unbelief and questioning doubts, and make shipwreck of faith.[3]

The disparity in faith and belief between the ten spies, who reported that the Israelites could not possess the land of Canaan, as opposed to Joshua and Caleb, who said it was possible with God, depended on one's attitude toward God. Belief in God is a choice. Dr. Timothy Jennings says, "When we exercise the will and freely choose what is right, God imbues the mind with the divine energy that provides the strength necessary to break free from destructive patterns of living."[4] Once we sincerely and genuinely yield ourselves to God, He works in us to exercise our faith in Him. That is not possible with unbelief because it presents a persistent and stubborn opposition to God. Because Caleb and Joshua believed God, they were the only two of the older generation (apart from the Levites) whom God allowed to enter the Promised Land (Numbers 14).

Unbelief is very detestable to God. Anything that prevents us from exercising our faith in God is terrible. When we do not trust people, we cannot establish a healthy relationship with them. It is the same with God. Without faith in the Lord, we cannot have an intimate relationship with Him. To an unbelieving heart, all the promises of God mean nothing. Unbelief hinders us from enjoying the full benefits of all the good things that God has promised to us (Mark 11:22–24). That is not all. Unbelief prevents us from yielding ourselves to the Holy Spirit, whom God has sent to teach us His ways. The Helper reveals what is sinful in us and gives us the grace to repent and the power to overcome it. It is the Holy Spirit who provides us with the desire to yield and to obey God and to grow in faith. So, when we resist the imploring of the Spirit, we resist God Himself.

Unbelief blinds the person to the goodness and faithfulness of God. The children of Israel showed persistent unbelief despite God's presence in their midst, a pillar of cloud by day and a pillar of fire by night. God parted the Red Sea, and the people walked on dry land, while Pharaoh and his army perished in their sight. God fed them with manna and gave them water from the rock. But they still did not believe Him. "Then the LORD said to Moses, 'How long will these people treat me with contempt? How long will they refuse to believe in me, in spite of the signs I have performed among them?'" (Numbers 14:11, NIV). I wonder what questions the Lord poses about us today.

As Christians, God has promised us a paradise where there will be no pain, suffering, or death. And just like the Israelites, we need to exercise faith in God and allow Him to lead us home. The Lord desires that we trust Him in every situation because He is mighty, merciful, faithful, gracious, and just. Whatever God promises, He does.

Like any other evil or obstacle, the remedy for unbelief is spending time with the Lord through prayer, reading the Bible, and sharing what we learn with others. The more time we spend with God, the better we will know Him and believe. Our faith grows when we exercise it. Our love for Him gets more robust as we keep on allowing Him to reveal Himself to us. Our relationship with God enables us to overcome trials like Job did. Its fruit is shown especially during times of trials or hardship.

Let us pray for the grace to trust God and to exercise great faith in Him. If we have a keen desire to believe in the Lord, He will work a way for us to overcome our doubts. If we are willing, God will keep us away from the terrible sin of unbelief. Next, we will look at fear— another hindrance to surrender.

Chapter 4

Fear That Thwarts Surrender

The word fear refers to negative as well as positive emotions. The *Cambridge Dictionary* defines fear as a "strong emotion caused by great worry about something dangerous, painful, or unknown that is happening or might happen."[1] The Bible also refers to this kind of fear, especially regarding worry or anxiety. But when describing our attitude toward God, fear has a positive meaning. In that case, it refers to respect, honor, and obedience to the Lord. God told Moses, "Gather me the people together, and I will let them hear my words, that they may learn to fear me all the days they shall live upon the earth, and that they may teach their children" (Deuteronomy 4:10). Furthermore, Luke 1:50 says, "And His mercy is on those who fear Him from generation to generation."

God wants His people to fear Him—in other words, to willingly worship Him—serve Him and do His will, instead of doing whatever their sinful nature dictates. People who fear God do not dread Him. They love and respect Him so much that they want to please Him. They determine in their hearts to turn away from evil, and God gives them the grace to hate sin and the power to avoid it. His grace is available to all who want it.

The Bible teaches us to respect God highly and to regard His will above our own. While it is wise to avoid danger, especially when there is a threat, God gives stringent instructions for people not to allow fear to hinder them from giving their lives to Him or from doing His will. God wants His people to be courageous in pursuing His course. They should not allow fear to hold them hostage. "The fear of man brings a snare, But whoever trusts in the LORD shall be safe" (Proverbs 29:25). Another word for a snare is a trap. So if we allow fear to come between God and us, it becomes a snare that will trap us for destruction.

God is, absolutely, trustworthy: He wants us to trust Him and allow Him to lead us to enter into a loving relationship with Him and live a life of victory as Christians. Over and over again, the Bible tells us not to fear or be anxious about anything. Yet many times, Christians—just like non-Christians—succumb to all kinds of fear. Many things trigger our alarms. In October 2016, I attended a conference where I learned about the fear triggers discussed in the next section.

Fear of Witchcraft and Demonic Powers

When I first read about the conference, I wondered *why in the world would Andrews University hold a conference on witchcraft.* Upon attending and listening to several presenters, I realized that many church members—including some pastors—in various parts of Africa were too scared to confront witchcraft issues in their churches. Heads of theology departments in various universities in Africa and those from Andrews University talked about working on their curriculum to train pastors on how to deal with witchcraft. I sat there, asking myself why pastors would be too afraid to confront the witchcraft issues in their churches and communities?

Then I remembered that during my childhood in Makueni, Kenya, witches, and witch doctors were a familiar sight. One of our neighbors was a renowned witch doctor in the country. From the city of Nairobi and other provinces, people came for healing from sicknesses, undoing witch spells, or protection from witchcraft.

Pieces of sacrifices that the witch doctor used to destroy the spells and other operations would be strewn along the roads that we used when going to school. And people feared contracting sicknesses from contact with the pieces of sacrifices that the witch doctor scattered along their paths.

They believed that the first person to walk over the sacrificial pieces would contract the sickness or pick a bad omen that the witch doctors transferred from those who visited them, to the sacrifices themselves. Nonetheless, my mother told my siblings and me never to fear witches or witch doctors and their sacrifices. She said, "The God of Abraham, Isaac, and Jacob is more powerful than all witch doctors or witches. God is more powerful than Satan." So, even though we grew up hearing all sorts of stories concerning witchcraft, we were never bothered by them.

Understandably, when I saw speakers from various universities in Africa meet in the United States to discuss how to deal with the fear of witchcraft in churches, I initially had a problem believing it. But then I realized that not everyone had the same exposure as I had to witchcraft. And the situation was a wake-up call for me. I realized that I, too, had other kinds of threats that caused me to be afraid, and that, from time to time, I caught my breath as these threats crossed my mind. Besides witchcraft, people can fear sickness, poverty, terrorism, and a myriad of other situations that could lead to physical, emotional, and psychological damage.

Fear prevents many people from going the distance to serve God. Some people are so fearful that they cannot even share with others the truth from the Bible because they do not want to offend anyone. Others allow fear to prevent them from carrying out their duties in the church. However, Paul is an excellent example of someone who conquered fear and showed trust and confidence in God, even in the face of evil spirits. We read:

> Once when we were going to the place of prayer, we were met by a female slave who had a spirit by which she predicted the future. She earned a great deal of money for her owners by fortune-telling. She followed Paul and the rest of us, shouting, "These men are servants of the Most High God, who are telling you the way to be saved." She kept this up for many days. Finally Paul became so annoyed that he turned around and said to the spirit, "In the name of Jesus Christ I command you to come out of her!" At that moment the spirit left her. (Acts 16:16–18, NIV)

The young woman in these verses had an evil spirit that enabled her to foretell the future. If she had lived in my village, she would have been called a diviner because she assumed supernatural powers to foretell the future, part of what diviners do. But since Paul had the Spirit of God in him, he commanded the evil spirit to leave the girl. And the evil spirit left her. After that, she could no longer divine. Paul used the same power that Jesus used to drive off a legion of demons from the man Legion (Mark 5:1–20). The same power is available to any surrendered Christian today.

Apart from the power in the name of Jesus, no one needs any special powers to face witchcraft or other demonic forces. Growing up, I witnessed the burning of witchcraft paraphernalia from those who converted to Christianity and from Christians who stopped practicing witchcraft. I found it surprising that the exorcism of demons was carried out by simple folks—lay preachers and pastors with little education but who were empowered by the Holy Spirit. Once the people allowed Jesus Christ to come into their lives, they believed that God would protect them. And He did.

It works to trust in Jesus. If we pray for the Holy Spirit to fill our hearts, we will gain the power to lead people to Christ without the fear of witchcraft or other evils. Witches and wizards derive their power from Satan. Yet we know from Scripture that Jesus defeated Satan in heaven as well as on earth (Revelation 12:7-9; John 19:30). God makes it clear that Christians must be prepared to join the battle. Ellen White states, "The Lord does not deceive us. He does not say to us, 'Do not fear; there are no dangers in your path.' He knows that there are trials and dangers, and He deals with us plainly. He does not propose to take His people out of the world of sin and evil, but He points to a never-failing refuge."[2] We do not fight this battle alone. Christ leads us, and He gives us guidance on how to go about it. Ephesians 6:12 tells us, "For we do not wrestle against flesh and blood, but against principalities, against powers, against the rulers of the darkness of this age, against spiritual hosts of wickedness in the heavenly places." No pastor or any other Christian can face Satan with human power alone. But with Jesus, Satan and his hosts will flee.

Jesus said, "I say to you, if you have faith as a mustard seed, you will say to this mountain, 'Move from here to there,' and it will move; and nothing will be impossible for you" (Matthew 17:20). Yes, if we have faith, even as small as the size of a mustard seed, we will pray, and God will honor our prayers. Let us pray for the grace to believe that God can help us overcome any situation in life, including fear. "If you can believe, all things are possible to him that believes" (Mark 9:23). Jesus Himself said these words.

Double Allegiance

Fear causes people to practice double allegiance. That happens when, on the one hand, people worship God. On the other hand, they seek protection from ancestral spirits or other Satanic operations when faced with hardships like rejection, poverty, sickness, and even death. Those who practice double allegiance believe that God's power is not enough to rely on; they think that one must supplement God's power with other means.

Christians have no reason to allow fear to prevent them from putting all their trust in God, for the Lord can protect His people from any dangerous situation. But if God's will is to allow something we wouldn't like to happen to us, we should still let His will be done. If we do not surrender to God, we are sure to become victims of Satan. And even when we surrender to God, Satan never gives up. The only way out is for us to pray that the Holy Spirit empowers us to stay connected to Jesus.

Fear that separates people from God is sinful. "But the cowardly, unbelieving, abominable, murderers, sexually immoral, sorcerers, idolaters, and all liars shall have their part in the lake which burns with fire and brimstone, which is the second death" (Revelation 21:8). Anybody who will not give his or her life to God because of fear is a coward, and cowards will not inherit the kingdom of God. Yet, fear is a reality that even a Christian must reckon with and prayerfully and continuously fight. The strongest of Christians will sometimes fear. But fear should not separate us from God. We should not give up our faith because of fear. If we are willing to trust God and to follow Him, He will give us wisdom and knowledge on how to serve Him in every situation.

Prayer of Faith

Many years ago, I traveled from the capital city of Kenya, Nairobi, to visit my mother in the rural area. Instead of driving, I used public transportation. At the end of my visit, I got up at 5:00 a.m., when it was still dark. Then I joined a company of relatives who were also returning to Nairobi and other parts of the country. There was a debate about which route to take as we walked the long distance to catch a bus. One of my relatives suggested that we take a long way because rumor had it that evil spirits haunted the shortcut. Instead, I told them that if we prayed, Jesus would lead us. As a result, they suggested that I would be the one to lead the way. So we prayed and took the shortcut through the woods to the bus station without a problem.

Having faith in God's power to protect His own should not necessarily downplay the reality of evil forces. The battle is real. Whatever the case may be, we should know and believe that God has more power than Satan. If we have faith in God, we will experience God's power in our lives.

From experience, I know that without the protection of God, I would be dead. In March 1989, I took maternity leave from the university where I was studying. I went back to a secondary school in Kenya, where I had previously taught with my husband, David. Even though I had resigned from my job to pursue higher education, I went back to deliver our baby because my husband was still teaching at the school.

At the time, we lived on the school compound, and we used outdoor bathrooms situated on a high ground where we had to climb several stairs to access them. On the side of the stairs was a big dry tree that had fallen. It had branches with sharp ends sticking out. One day while going down the stairs, I felt like unseen hands were violently pushing me from behind. I went down fast on my stomach, facing the sharp, protruding tree branches on the ground. But to my surprise, I landed gently on my feet next to the fallen tree. I believed that Satan and his agents tried to attack me, but they failed.

Following our wedding in 1988, David and I often found all sorts of potions, dead birds, and other devilish paraphernalia outside our door. We always prayed, swept them away, and went on with life. But the physical attack on the day I was pushed could have killed my unborn child and me. From that experience, I learned not to take life for granted. We continued praying, and even though the devil did not give up instantly, he did eventually give us a break. That being said, the battle has continued in different ways over the years. Yes, the battle between good and evil–between Christ and Satan–is very real. But God never abandons us.

Whether we face the challenges of pride, unbelief, fear, sickness, rejection, poverty, or any other obstacle in our Christian life, we should always remember that the archenemy and the mastermind of all opposition to surrender to God is Satan. And he is a defeated foe. All we need to do is to surrender to Jesus and let Him fight for us. And as Ellen White states in *Steps to Christ,* "Keep your wants, joys, your sorrows, your cares, and your fears before God. You cannot burden Him… His heart of love is touched by our sorrows, and even by our utterances of them. Take to Him everything that perplexes the mind. Nothing is too great for Him to bear, for He holds up worlds."[3] Let us trust God. He is able.

Without God's power, even the best Christian is no match for the devil. As humans, we are weak, but Satan is no match for our Savior, Jesus Christ. Our Lord is much, much, stronger than Satan. God is ever-ready to fight our spiritual battles for us, but He wants us to allow Him to do so willingly. Let us not allow fear to separate us from Christ. Let us surrender ourselves to the Lord, and He will give us victory over all the evil that the devil uses to separate us from God.

Chapter 5

Blessings for the Surrendered

Once people surrender themselves to God, they become His children. And God takes charge of their lives. He gives them the power to overcome sin and to serve Him. The blessings for the surrendered include forgiveness of sins, grace to love God and humanity, happiness, peace, joy, and high assurance of eternal life. In this chapter, we will see several of God's people who received great blessings from Him.

I learn a lot from the experience of Abraham, whom God called to move from his country to a place where the Lord would show him. Abraham obeyed and committed his life entirely to God. Then he left Haran for Canaan. Later, God made a covenant with him that the patriarch kept all his life.

Two things intrigue me most about the relationship between God and Abraham. One is the faithfulness of God to Abraham, which manifests itself in many ways, such as the miracles that the Lord performed to fulfill His promises to Abraham. After being barren and past menopause, Abraham's wife, Sarah, bore Isaac, who became heir of the promise. Everywhere Abraham went, blessings followed him. Even when a drought hit Canaan, Abraham and Sarah went to Egypt and lived there with lots of animals and servants.

Whenever Abraham got into trouble, God was always there for Him. For example, I love the grace and the faithfulness of God in the two incidents when both Pharaoh and Abimelech tried to take

Sarah for a wife. In each case, Abraham and his wife agreed to misrepresent their relationship by saying that Sarah was his sister. Indeed, Sarah was Abraham's stepsister, but they told a half-truth because they did not say that she was also his wife. Abraham knew that Sarah was so beautiful that the kings would want to take her for a wife. Sure enough, they tried. But God would not let them have Sarah. So, He intervened in both cases. Pharaoh and his people suffered terrible plagues. When Pharaoh realized the reason for the suffering, he sent Sarah back to Abraham. As for Abimelech, God spoke to him in a dream and warned him of imminent death if he did not give her back to Abraham. And just like Pharaoh, Abimelech sent her back to Abraham (Genesis 20). God is such a "Dad," always merciful and ready to help His children.

Second, I find the faith of Abraham in God not only fascinating but also exemplary. Abraham's faith seems to have continued to grow as he interacted with God. The same Abraham who told half-truths twice and tried to "help" God by getting a child through Sarah's maid, Hagar, is the same one who almost sacrificed his son, Isaac. That level of faith and trust in God is incredible, utterly exemplary.

I find God's relationship with Abraham deeply encouraging for us today. God remained faithful to his human friend through it all. Abraham believed in God's goodness and faithfulness. And God honored Abraham's faith. The Lord protected and provided for all Abraham's needs. We are told, "Now Abraham was old, well advanced in age; and the LORD had blessed Abraham in all things" (Genesis 24:1). Imagine if that sentence were to be said about you. Visualize, if, at the end of your life, people would say that you lived a long life and that God blessed you in all things. Wow! God's love and faithfulness are forever available to any person who puts his or her life and trust totally in Him. Scripture tells us, "For the Lord God is a sun and shield; The Lord will give grace and glory; No good thing will He withhold from those who walk uprightly" (Psalm 84:11). What a blessing it is to surrender oneself to the Lord, the God of heaven!

Endurance and Peace in the Storms of Life

"God's grace is ever with His people no matter what happens to them. As long as you live, put yourself in God's hands and be strong and courageous because tough times happen to anybody at any time," David's grandmother told me these words. At the time, I had gone to console her after losing her son and her husband a few months apart. I thought that must have been a challenging time in her life, and yet when I arrived at her home, she was calm. As I admired her peace and strength, I imagined how differently she might have been talking if she did not know God.

I have remembered grandma's words many times in my life. And between 2015 and the end of 2017, something happened that taught me that for sure, God's grace is ever with His people no matter what happens to them. During that time, I was pursuing my Ph.D., and I came to the point where I needed to collect data for my dissertation. By then, I had completed writing my proposal, which my dissertation committee approved, and the university Institutional Review Board (IRB) had permitted me to proceed to data collection.

My proposal stated that I was going to collect data from a particular group of schools in Texas. But when I sent my request to the superintendent, it took much explanation and convincing before I was granted permission on the condition that the school principals gave their consent. For some reason, when I sent my request to the principals, over three-quarters of them declined. I did everything I could to increase participation to no avail. I needed at least 100 participants for my study. But by the end of two semesters, I had only 26. My dissertation committee told me that my participants were too few, so I could not complete my study. I made a few changes to increase the number of participants, but it did not help.

My last option was to go out of the country to collect data. But my dissertation committee said, “No.” I thought this was the end of my dream to attain a Ph.D., and the thought of quitting after spending thousands of dollars was alarming. By then, I had completed 76 credit hours of coursework. I could not stand the idea of giving up when I was so close to the end. Yet, I was out of options.

When it seemed like all hope was lost, I went home from college and told God to let His will be done. I continued praying, waiting to see what the Lord would do. It was during that time that I got reminded about the blessing of trusting God. Even though I felt frustrated by the turn of events, I still placed my hope in God. I prayed, *Lord, I asked You to open the way for me to go back to school for a Ph.D. You opened the door, and You faithfully led me to this point. I do not believe that You will leave me with the project halfway done, after spending so much time and money in the program so far. I do not know how to go back at this point. Father, God of heaven, please, make a way for me to get enough data, and give me a testimony. In Jesus' name, I pray, Amen.*

After that prayer, I stayed home without knowing how I was going to solve the problem. I put it in God's hands and left it there completely. He was going to make a way for me, or I would drop out of my program after all the years, money, and opportunity cost.

Then the Lord did what only God could do. Two months from when I prayed, I got data from more than 5,000 participants from all over North America. As if getting the data and completing my Ph.D. program was not enough, I defended my dissertation on December 14, 2017. And on March 29, 2018, I was given a chance and financial support to present the study at a conference.

The hope and peace that I experienced during that tough time reminded me, yet again, about the blessing of putting my faith in God. Every time I look at my dissertation, I thank God that I failed to get the 100 participants from Texas. The way God provided the solution to that problem is a constant encouragement to trust Him. "All things work together for good to those who love God, to those who are the called according to His purpose" (Romans 8:28). The Bible presents plenty of stories about people whose lives changed completely for good after they surrendered to God. They received power to overcome evil and to serve God.

Earlier we read about Paul's commitment to God, especially after his conversion. This chapter focuses on his blessings as a result of his surrender to the Savior, Jesus Christ. Before his submission to the Lord, Paul was like a madman. Scripture tells us,

> Then Saul, still breathing threats and murder against the disciples of the Lord, went to the high priest and asked letters from him to the synagogues of Damascus, so that if he found any who were of the Way, whether men or women, he might bring them bound to Jerusalem. As he journeyed he came near Damascus, and suddenly a light shone around him from heaven. Then he fell to the ground and heard a voice saying to him, "Saul, Saul, why are you persecuting Me?" And he said, "Who are You, Lord?" Then the Lord said, "I am Jesus, whom you are persecuting. It is hard for you to kick against the goads." So he, trembling and astonished, said, "Lord, what do You want me to do?" Then the Lord said to him, "Arise and go into the city, and you will be told what you must do." (Acts 9:1–6)

Before his conversion, Paul, who was known as Saul at the time, persecuted Christians. But unlike Judas, who just confessed that Jesus was innocent but failed to repent and surrender, Paul humbled himself and surrendered totally to the Lord. He asked the Lord for instructions on what to do. And whatever Jesus instructed him to do, he did.

Instead of insisting on his way, Paul learned to submit to God daily. He prayed for power to do the work that God sent him to do. Without divine power and grace to change the mind and heart, no human being can get converted. Surrender is crucial. After Paul surrendered himself into God's hands, he stopped persecuting Christians and experienced peace. Surrendered Christians are peaceful people because they have hope. Regardless of what happens in this life, God can give His people peace.

In addition, surrendering one's heart and mind to Christ keeps one safe from the enemy. Satan takes possession of those who reject God. The story of Judas Iscariot shows the unfortunate situation of failure to yield one's heart to the Savior. Judas followed Jesus physically as if he was one with the Lord. However, his actions and the things that he spoke showed otherwise. Scripture tells us, "But one of His disciples, Judas Iscariot, Simon's son, who would betray Him, said, 'Why was this fragrant oil not sold for three hundred denarii and given to the poor?' This he said, not that he cared for the poor, but because he was a thief, and had the money box; and he used to take what was put in it" (John 12:4–6). What a terrible description of one who followed Jesus for at least three years.

Like the other disciples, Judas Iscariot had the opportunity he needed to surrender his life to Christ and to become a great preacher of the good news to the world. He walked with Jesus and witnessed all the miracles the Savior performed. He heard the sermons that Jesus preached in public and in private. But instead of yielding his heart to the Savior, Judas chose to put on the appearance of a disciple. He pretended to be one of the Savior's followers while he worked for Satan. And when Peter wondered where he and the other disciples would go, apart from to Jesus, "Jesus answered them, 'Did

I not choose you, the twelve, and one of you is a devil?'" (John 6:70). Mercy! Judas gave the enemy a chance to inspire and destroy him.

While Christ displayed a sincere love for them all, Judas stuck to his selfishness. He valued earthly possessions more than the Savior and at the expense of his soul. Even though Judas followed Jesus, he never allowed himself to learn from the Savior. Judas never let Jesus change and empower him to overcome evil. "Then Satan entered Judas, surnamed Iscariot, who was numbered among the twelve" (Luke 22:3). Satan could not have entered the heart of Judas by force. Had Judas given his whole heart to Christ, the devil would not have had such victory over him. Dr. Timothy R. Jennings posits, "When we understand the truth about God and His methods and surrender to Him, a new motive- set of principles/ methods become the governing power in the human mind, removing "sin" (the rebellious selfish method)."[1] Those who surrender fully to God receive everything they need to participate successfully in the battle between good and evil. The surrendered receive power to accomplish everything that God desires for them. Hence, they bring God great glory by allowing Him to use them to save others.

Jesus said, "Most assuredly, I say to you, he who believes in Me, the works that I do he will do also; and greater works than these he will do, because I go to My Father" (John 14:12). The works that Jesus did on earth included healing people such as those possessed by demons, lepers, and resurrecting the dead. He also fed thousands of people miraculously.

Did Jesus mean that those who believe in Him will do great works as He did? Absolutely. Those who accept Jesus Christ and allow Him to dwell in them become instruments through which the Lord performs great works of saving the lost. The apostle Peter's ministry is an excellent example of the power the surrendered have to do great jobs as Jesus did on earth. Among the miracles that Peter performed included healing the paralyzed like Aeneas, who had been in bed for eight years.

"And Peter said to him, 'Aeneas, Jesus the Christ heals you. Arise and make your bed.' Then he arose immediately" (Acts 9:34). And he was healed. In the same chapter, we see that Dorcas, who selflessly helped widows, died after being sick. Then Peter restored her to life through the power of prayer (verse 40). Indeed, those who surrender themselves fully to the Lord get empowered to be powerful in God's hands.

Jesus said that whoever believes in Him, "greater works than these he will do." The *Seventh-day Adventist Bible Commentary,* on the book of John, tells us that the work of the disciples of Jesus will be "greater in quantity rather than quality. Christ's activity had extended over a relatively small area of the world. After the ascension, the gospel would spread to all parts of the world." [2] Through the workings of the Holy Spirit, God's people are leading multitudes to the Savior throughout the world. There are still many who need to be taught about the gospel of Jesus Christ in our neighborhoods.

You and I can be as powerful as Peter in whatever ministry God gives us. It is a lack of faith in God, and sin that makes people be like "toy Christians"—powerless. But that needs not to be the case because, in Jesus, we have forgiveness of sin and grace to get into the state of the blessed person described in Psalm 1, who has the power to resist evil. And the person is so blessed that he or she is like a tree planted beside a river with plenty of water. Whatever the person does prosper. Better still, the surrendered have eternal life waiting for them. Will you surrender your life entirely to the Lord and enjoy the special blessings both in this world and in the world to come?

Chapter 6

The Time Factor

If you have ever missed a plane or a bus or failed to register for a semester course because it was too late, then you know what I mean by the time factor—failing to meet deadlines, after which people cannot get what they need. Let me tell you about one of my experiences with the time factor. During my undergraduate days, I realized that I could have one history class waived instead of doing two as a general requirement. I approached the department chair, who promised that if I produced the right documents, I could get the second history class waived. I knew that I qualified for the benefit, so I focused on other courses, trying to finish all my degree requirements so that I could graduate at the end of the semester.

As I waited to produce my documents to get the class waived, I received news that the chair of the history department had been involved in a road accident and was in the hospital. I remember feeling so sorry for the department chair and very concerned about not completing my course as planned. I knew that unless the professor recovered and returned to college soon, I might not be able to graduate that year because I would have to wait for someone else to take the chair's place to complete the process of waiving the course. Then I remembered a saying my mother tells people: "Mbaa ngeeka meethiiwe mataneka," meaning those who procrastinate and say, "I'll do it later" seldom get things done.

Even in matters of salvation, time is crucial because people can only yield their hearts to the Savior while they live. Dead people do not have a chance to accept or to reject Jesus Christ as their Savior and Lord of their lives. "The dead know nothing" (Ecclesiastes, 9:5). A dead person cannot make a decision or act on anything. I cannot overemphasize the reality that it is only in this life that we have a chance to believe in Christ to receive everlasting life.

Because the Lord understands the importance of the time factor in our salvation, Scripture tells us, "Today, if you will hear his voice, harden not your hearts as in the rebellion" (Hebrews 3:15). God gives human beings lots of chances to give their lives to Him and to remain in His hands. Indeed, He is incredibly gracious and longsuffering. When we repent our sins, He forgives us. The Lord knows when we do not yet understand enough to surrender to Him. So, the Holy Spirit keeps on revealing truths to us, leading us to repentance and surrender. In the same way, the Lord knows when we hear His Word, understand the message, but choose to either reject Him or to push our commitment to sometime in the future. Surrender is a deliberate decision that a person makes.

Many people would like to live with God in paradise forever. When they hear or read about heaven, they praise God because, there, love, peace, joy, and life will never end. When Jesus comes, He will eradicate death. We will live forever without any sickness, pain, or hatred. Many admire that life. But some have cherished sins they are not ready to forsake just yet; hence, they say, "One day, I will give up all for Jesus." But who knows what will happen tomorrow?

You know how uncertain and short life on earth can be if you have ever heard or known someone who died in an accident. The Psalmist entreated God, "So teach us to number our days, that we may gain a heart of wisdom" (Psalm 90:12). The Psalmist must have realized that life on earth passes like the wind. There is a short time between childhood and old age. It looks like people leave the world before they live.

The Danger of Procrastination

Sudden death is not the only danger of delaying to give our hearts entirely to God. Ellen White tells us,

> Beware of procrastination. Do not put off the work of forsaking your sins and seeking purity of heart through Jesus. Here is where thousands upon thousands have erred to their eternal loss. I will not here dwell upon the shortness and uncertainty of life; but there is a terrible danger—a danger not sufficiently understood—in delaying to yield to the pleading voice of God's Holy Spirit, in choosing to live in sin; for such this delay really is. Sin, however small it may be esteemed, can be indulged in only at the peril of infinite loss. What we do not overcome will overcome us and work out our destruction... Every act of transgression, every neglect or rejection of the grace of Christ, is reacting upon yourself; it is hardening the heart, depraving the will, benumbing the understanding, and not only making you less inclined to yield, but less capable of yielding, to the tender pleading of God's Holy Spirit.[1]

It is a sobering fact that people can reach a point where they cannot repent their sins. Paul says that these people are "past feeling," and "have given themselves over to lewdness, to work all uncleanness with greediness" (Ephesians 4:19). It is very dangerous to keep on resisting the pleadings of the Holy Spirit.

If a person knows the right thing to do but chooses to act contrary to the will of God continually, there comes a time when sin ceases to bother that person. Then the person sins continuously without repenting and turning away from sin, which leads to death. "His own iniquities entrap the wicked man, And he is caught in the cords of his sin" (Proverbs 5:22). Reaching the point where a person is unable to yield to the Holy Spirit of God is another form of dying.

God does not want any person to be lost. Hence, His Holy Spirit keeps talking to us to yield to the Lord while we can, either before one is physically dead or before one reaches the point where he or she cannot respond to the Holy Spirit, without whom nobody repents. God is perfect in His judgments. Those who sin out of ignorance or weakness find forgiveness. But those who deliberately choose to reject Him or refuse His will are the ones who go "past feeling" and are unable to repent and find forgiveness.

The Right Time

To emphasize the importance of time in our salvation, Jesus said,

> But of that day and hour no one knows, not even the angels of heaven, but My Father only. But as the days of Noah were, so also will the coming of the Son of Man be. For as in the days before the flood, they were eating and drinking, marrying and giving in marriage, until the day that Noah entered the ark, and did not know until the flood came and took them all away, so also will the coming of the Son of Man be. (Matthew 24:36–39)

Jesus reminded His hearers of the experience of Noah and the people of that time, and how Noah preached for 120 years while the people ignored him. They heard the voice of Noah talking about the rain that would destroy the world. They heard Noah's voice inviting them to build the ark and to get inside before the door was shut. Instead of listening and acting on God's warning, they chose to continue with their lifestyle.

The Bible tells us that the people were wicked. Yet, God gave them a chance to repent and turn to Him through the preaching of Noah. Unfortunately, they refused to learn and realize that their time was running out. By the time they made up their minds to take Noah's offer and get into the ark, it was too late. God had already shut the door. The time factor caught up with them.

Jesus used Noah's illustration to compare it to His second coming. Just as the people of Noah's time got busy with their lives, eating and drinking, marrying and giving in marriage, Jesus will come back on earth and find many unprepared to go to heaven with Him. You may ask, what was wrong with eating, drinking, marrying, and giving in marriage? Indeed, there is nothing wrong with these activities, as long as they are done according to God's instructions. Scripture provides guidelines. The problem was that the people did not only get preoccupied with the activities in their daily lives, but also planned evil, such as corruption and violence, and implemented it (Genesis 6). Then God sent Noah to warn them, but they scorned Noah and continued with their lives as usual.

Jesus said that during the last days, history will repeat itself. The same attitudes and the same focus on worldly cares with no regard for God that dominated people's attention during Noah's time will be present just before Jesus comes back. How many people in the world today have heard the gospel of Jesus Christ for decades but have decided to turn a deaf ear? Some go to church but are not serious about their Christianity. Jesus said that many would be found in that same state—living in their sins. I am glad that the Word of God tells us in advance that nobody is going to repent in heaven. What a precious opportunity we have today!

Since Jesus said that, apart from the Father, nobody knows the time of His coming, we have only one safe option: to be ready for our Lord. To stay surrendered to God is the safest situation to be in so that whether we die before Jesus comes back or whether the Lord comes back while we are still alive, we are ready to go with Him to heaven. You and I have a golden opportunity to surrender to God right now that we are still alive. Now is the time to pray, "Lord God of heaven, come into my heart and change me. Enable me to do your will, to live for you and to serve you wholly. In Jesus' name, I pray. Amen." Will you join me in this prayer?

God promises not to deny us any good thing (Psalm 84:11). When we give ourselves entirely to Him, we are not going to miss any good thing. The things that God wants us to avoid are those that are going to separate us from Him. He is the source of our life. True happiness, fulfillment, and joy come from our connection with our God and Creator. Because He created us, He knows what is best for us. For that reason, our surrender to Him is a gain, not a loss. The sooner we do it, the better it is for us. From that point on, we are free to call on God with confidence and ask for whatever we desire. As long as it is a good thing, and according to His will, He will give it to us.

Jesus said, "But seek first the kingdom of God and His righteousness, and all these things shall be added to you" (Matthew 6:33). Once we put God first in our lives, we can confidently give Him our cares. He promises to give us the desires of our hearts. In His wisdom, the Lord advises us not to procrastinate our total surrender to Him. I pray that you yield your heart to Him now. Will you?

Chapter 7

Allowing God's Will to Be Done in You

The essence of total surrender to God is to allow His will to be done in our lives. Jeremiah tells us,

> The word which came to Jeremiah from the LORD, saying: "Arise and go down to the potter's house, and there I will cause you to hear My words." Then I went down to the potter's house, and there he was, making something at the wheel. And the vessel that he made of clay was marred in the hand of the potter; so he made it again into another vessel, as it seemed good to the potter to make. Then the word of the LORD came to me, saying: "O house of Israel, can I not do with you as this potter?" Says the Lord. (Jeremiah 18:1–6)

If the Lord asks me whether He can do with my life what the potter did with the clay, will I say "Yes" without hesitation? Will you?

God wants us to trust Him enough to let Him do with our lives whatever He deems fit. But many of us have plans for our lives, and we want to pursue them to the end. That is one of the areas for which I pray most in my life. I am very grateful that the Bible gives us plenty of examples from which to learn. For instance, I learn a great lesson about God's will from the life of Joseph.

God's Will

Joseph became a slave in Egypt, and later a prisoner accused of a crime that he never committed. The young man found himself in a predicament in Potiphar's house, but he had the integrity and determination to do God's will in a tough situation. Genesis 39:7–10 tells us:

> And it came to pass after these things that his master's wife cast longing eyes on Joseph, and she said, "Lie with me." But he refused and said to his master's wife, "Look, my master does not know what is with me in the house, and he has committed all that he has to my hand… How then can I do this great wickedness, and sin against God?" So it was, as she spoke to Joseph day by day, that he did not heed her, to lie with her or to be with her.

The Bible tells us that Joseph was only 17 when his brothers sold him into slavery. But look at the question that he asked his master's wife: "How then can I do this great wickedness, and sin against God?" Joseph desired to do the will of God, and he pursued it at the expense of his job and freedom. We know that Joseph ended up in prison for refusing to lie with Potiphar's wife. She accused him of attempted rape. What impresses me most about Joseph is his attitude toward God during those difficult times and later toward his brothers. After many years, the brothers found Joseph in Egypt, not as a slave but the Prime Minister of the country:

> And Joseph said to his brothers, "Please come near to me." So they came near. Then he said: "I am Joseph your brother, whom you sold into Egypt. But now, do not therefore be grieved or angry with yourselves because you sold me here; for God sent me before you to preserve life. For these two years the famine

> has been in the land, and there are still five years in which there will be neither plowing nor harvesting. And God sent me before you to preserve a posterity for you in the earth, and to save your lives by a great deliverance. So now it was not you who sent me here, but God; and He has made me a father to Pharaoh, and lord of all his house, and a ruler throughout all the land of Egypt." (Genesis 45:4–8)

The *Seventh-day Adventist Bible Commentary*, on the book of Genesis, tells us, "Joseph repeated his former assertion, that it was God who had sent him to Egypt for a definite purpose. He spoke prophetically here, to the effect that God had brought him to Egypt in order to preserve through him the family destined to become God's chosen people, by delivering them from starvation."[1] Talk about God's grace! Remember, before Joseph's brothers sold him into slavery, he had two dreams that pointed to his future greatness.

The dreams showed that the whole family, including his father and brothers, would bow to him one day. When Joseph shared his dreams with the family, Jacob, his father, rebuked him, and his brothers hated him even more. The Bible tells us that despite admonishing Joseph, Jacob kept the dreams in his mind.

Now, imagine Joseph in prison. Surely the dreams did not prepare him for that. How was he able to avoid the confusion, and sometimes bitterness, that goes with delayed promises? Have you ever built all your hope on a commitment or a pledge? What happens when it fails? Joseph was experiencing something worse than a delayed promise. He was dealing with a terrible situation that he never expected at all. Remember, he was his father's favorite child. So his experience in Egypt before he got promoted to the Prime Minister position must have been challenging. But his words to his brothers show us that he realized that God was in charge of his life. Whatever happened to him, God allowed it for a good reason. It is incredible that after all the suffering, Joseph's choice of words and focus portray his gladness that God used him to accomplish His purpose. Joseph's attitude provides an excellent example of allowing God's will in one's life.

Despite the circumstances, Joseph was peaceful because he realized that God was in control. That's why he told his brothers that it was God who sent him to Egypt. And it was God who placed him in the position of power throughout Egypt. Joseph trusted in God's goodness regardless of his suffering from the hatred of his brothers, suffering in Potiphar's house and later in prison. He was at peace with it all because he believed that his life fulfilled the will of God.

Then, after Jacob had passed away, Joseph assured his brothers that they had nothing to fear. He was not going to get revenge for what they did to him. Joseph told them that the evil that they planned for him when they sold him into slavery turned out to be a blessing to many. He said that God allowed it for a purpose. That attitude toward God's will for his life is exemplary.

Of all the examples we can give about allowing the will of God in our lives, Jesus Christ is the best. In the Garden of Gethsemane, Jesus prayed to the Father to let the cup, dying on the cross, pass Him. But then He asked for the Father's will to be done. It amazes me that Christ chose to go through such a painful death to honor God's will. What makes the case of Jesus more special is that He was sinless, and He had the power to avoid the cross, yet He chose to humble Himself and surrender to God's will.

The story of Joseph and that of Jesus are examples of people who suffered a lot without deserving it. But unlike them, there are many times when our choices in life put us in painful situations. We experience the consequences. Even then, our attitudes should be like King David's when Prophet Nathan confronted him about taking Uriah's wife. David confessed his sin and faced the consequences of his choices with humility.

We may not be sold into slavery like Joseph, but we may face other trials and temptations in various ways. In whatever situation we find ourselves, let us allow the will of God in our lives. Only the Lord can make it possible.

One of the conditions that almost killed me strengthened me spiritually. At eight months of pregnancy, my unborn child stopped moving. An ultrasound showed that the fetus was dead. Doctors, relatives, and friends were terrified for my life. When I delivered the in-womb dead fetus with no pain killers, I was afraid that I would die due to physical and emotional pain. After the delivery, doctors said that the child had been dead for at least three days. Even though my life was in danger, it was the emotional pain that weighed so heavily on me. *Why did God let this happen?* This question has lingered on my mind for the last 20 years since I lost my baby. And up to this day, I do not know the answer.

As Christians, we ask ourselves such questions many times in our lives. But the response that we give ourselves depends on our relationship with God. During such times, your trust in God becomes crucial because you still need to hope in His goodness. You still need to turn to Him as a loving Father. With all the physical, emotional, and psychological trauma, I was able to cry to God as would a helpless child who trusted in the goodness of a loving parent. Even though I did not understand why, I believed that God still had the best interest for me. After I regained enough physical strength to walk and peace to go back to my normal life, I felt as if I had enough courage and trust in God to face any problem in life.

At the end of it all, I had much for which to thank God. The in-womb dead fetus could have led to severe health conditions for me. The crude process of delivery could have killed me. I dealt with low hemoglobin for several years. But what is that compared to the fact that I was alive? In every situation, God wants us to thank Him. If we believe that He is kind, merciful, and loving, we will thank Him for everything, good or bad. Without His grace, this is not possible.

If suffering comes our way, let us endure. James counsels us to learn about suffering and patience from the prophets who spoke for

God (James 5:7–11). You would expect them not to suffer at all. But no, they knew suffering in the most profound sense of the word. “Therefore let those who suffer according to the will of God commit their souls to Him in doing good, as to a faithful Creator” (1 Peter 4:19). Yes, let the will of God be done in our lives.

Even when we don't understand what is happening in our lives, let us remember that “all things work together for good to those who love God, to those who are the called according to His purpose” (Romans 8:28). To the surrendered Christians, those who love God, all things will work together for their good. No matter how bad your situation may look, God is always in control. He has allowed your position for a reason.

God’s Will for His Children

Let us pray for grace as we tell the Lord, “Let Your will be done in my life.” The Word of God presents to us the revealed will of God. As Christians, we know that it is God's will for us not to kill, steal, commit adultery, or to break any other commandment. When we allow the Holy Spirit to dwell in our hearts, He gives us wisdom, discernment and reveals God's will for us in every situation of our lives. Always, let's remember that God wants the best for us. “For I know the plans I have for you,” declares the LORD, “plans to prosper you and not to harm you, plans to give you hope and a future” (Jeremiah 29:11 NIV). God is faithful. Let us trust Him and hold on to Him. When we surrender ourselves to Him, we get grace to rejoice always, to pray without ceasing, and to give thanks for everything because we know that our faithful God is in control of our lives.

The best position in life is to be surrendered fully to God and to allow His will into our lives. Let us pray for the grace to cooperate with God.

Chapter 8

Transformation

Among the many synonyms for transformation are conversion and rebuilding. I am referring to a spiritual metamorphosis. Our faithful Lord brings the change in us. And for transformation to take place, we need to realize our need and cooperate with the Lord. Otherwise, we will behave like one professor in my college whom students accused of insulting them. During an assembly where the professor addressed students and faculty, he said something that most students found offensive. As a result, a group of student leaders convinced the rest of the students that the professor needed to apologize.

When the majority bought the idea, they managed to win the remaining few students. All the students sat in the auditorium, refusing to attend classes unless the professor apologized. When the administration realized that the students were serious, they persuaded the professor to apologize. Then when it was time for the apology, the majority of the faculty and administration came to the auditorium too.

The awaited time came for the professor to deliver the demanded apology, and he stood up and said something close to this, "I hear that I insulted students. I did not insult anybody, but I'm sorry for those who believe that I insulted them." And he sat down. I was one of the students in the auditorium. But even though I did not know much about the professor, for he did not teach in my department, I believed that he did not apologize. And I would not be surprised if he insulted the students again because he did not see the big deal about using the words and the tone that had put him in his current position. Real transformation requires a contrite heart.

A Change of Heart

King David is an excellent example of someone who sincerely desired to have a genuine change of heart to God's glory. By the time he prayed for the change in his life, David had presented an example of how miserably a human being can fail and fall into some of the most grievous sins ever committed. I mean, it cannot get worse than taking somebody's wife and organizing for her husband to be killed. But David repented in bitter tears. The king knew remorse in the most profound sense of the word. His repentance was so real that he asked God to change him from the inside out.

First of all, David admitted his sin. He said, "For I acknowledge my transgressions, And my sin is always before me. Against You, You only, have I sinned And done this evil in Your sight" (Psalm 51:3, 4). Repentance, which leads to transformation, starts with realizing and admitting that one is a sinner. That's why David prayed, "Wash me thoroughly from my iniquity and cleanse me from my sin" (verse 2).

Along with acknowledging his sinfulness, asking for forgiveness, and cleansing, David asked for the remedy of sin in his life. He prayed, "Create in me a clean heart, O God, And renew a steadfast spirit within me. Do not cast me away from Your presence, And do not take Your Holy Spirit from me" (verses 10, 11). The king prayed for transformation from his sinful, immoral self to a godly man filled with the Spirit of God. What about us?

Every Surrendered Christian

Scripture tells us that there should be an evident change in the life of every true believer. "When you heard about Christ and were taught in him according with the truth that is in Jesus. You were taught, with regard to your former way of life, to put off your old self, which is being corrupted by its deceitful desires; to be made new in the attitudes of your minds; and to put on the new self, created to be like God in true righteousness and holiness" (Ephesians 4:21–24, NIV). Once we are born again in Christ, God expects us to live as new creatures (2 Corinthians 5:17). Our attitudes toward God, self, and others change. That change shows in every aspect of our lives.

When our spiritual transformation takes place, we love God and honor Him in our thoughts, speech, and in all we do. We become humble, and we love others. In *Steps to Christ*, White posits that for us to get transformed to the image of God, "the whole heart must be yielded to God, or the change can never be wrought in us by which we are to be restored to His likeness."[1] Thus, our total surrender to the Lord is necessary for transformation to take place. We need the Holy Spirit to dwell in our hearts to teach, guide, and empower us continually. Then we will be able to overcome sin and reflect God to others for His glorify.

If there is no change at all in our lives compared to before and after we accept Jesus Christ as our Savior, then therein stands a problem; something is not right. The Word of God tells us that we should not live like those who have not yet given their lives to the Lord. And come to think of it, how can a true Christian's life be the same as the life of the people who chose to alienate themselves from God? Yet, many churchgoers have religion, but in whom Christ does not exist. Many people have spent years in churches, and even though they are baptized members, there is no difference between how they were before and after they started going to church.

When it comes to keeping God's commandments or dealing with other people, they hold the same attitudes as before they gained their religion. Paul describes them as, "lovers of themselves, lovers of money, boasters, proud, blasphemers, disobedient to parents, unthankful, unholy, unloving, unforgiving, slanderers, without self-control, brutal, despisers of good, traitors, headstrong, haughty, lovers of pleasure rather than lovers of God, having a form of godliness but denying its power" (2 Timothy 3:2–5). It is scary to have a form of godliness but deny its power, having an outward show of religion, but not having a converted heart. That is a condition the apostle Paul noticed with some who claimed to be followers of Christ. And it is a condition of some who call themselves Christians today. These people have no love for God or their fellow humans. They are satisfied with the outward show. They do not have the Holy Spirit in them. So, they have no relationship with Christ.

Through the help of the Holy Spirit, God's people learn from the Bible. The Spirit teaches them about Jesus Christ and the ways of truth. Scripture tells us that the Holy Spirit teaches people to put off their former conduct that stems from deceitful lusts.

Renewing of the Mind

God does not leave us to figure out how to bring change in our lives. The Lord does not only tell or show us what to do but also works in us to bring about the desired change if we let Him. According to William Hendriksen, "What is needed is transformation, inner change, the renewing of the mind, that is, not only of the organ of thinking and reasoning but of the inner disposition; better still of the heart, the inner being."[2] When the Holy Spirit works on our minds and hearts, our desires are directed to the will of God. Thus our minds get renewed. Transformation requires us to be real with God. We must mean business and honestly pray for God to change us from day-to-day. The more we prayerfully read the Word of God and pray, the more we are transformed to be like Christ. Ellen White gives a clear picture of the change that takes place in our lives when we allow Christ to work in our lives:

> The Spirit of God, received into the soul, will quicken all its faculties. Under the guidance of the Holy Spirit, the mind that is devoted unreservedly to God, develops harmoniously, and is strengthened to comprehend and fulfill the requirements of God. The weak, vacillating character becomes changed to one of strength and steadfastness. Continual devotion establishes so close a relation between Jesus and His disciples that the Christian becomes like Him in mind and character. Through a connection with Christ, he will have a clearer and broader view. His discernment will be more penetrative, his judgment better balanced. [3]

God is awesome. The Lord starts to work in us after we accept Jesus Christ as our Savior and Lord of our lives. The surrendered seek the Lord with all their hearts. Psalm 1 calls those people blessed. They keep God's commandments, but not by their power. Neither do they keep the law to be saved? They obey God's commandments because Christ saved them, and because God enables them to do it. Total surrender to the Lord takes care of it all.

The surrendered Christian grows spiritually. We continue to grow and to change to be like Christ throughout our lives if we remain in Him. In that process, we bear fruit; we serve God and bring Him glory. For us to stay connected to our Savior and Lord, we need to allow Him to live in us, in the form of the Holy Spirit.

Then our thinking is guided by God, who also enables us to seek His will in every situation.

Let us learn a lesson from the blessed person in Psalm 1:1, 2, who "walks not in the counsel of the ungodly, nor stands in the way of sinners, nor sits in the seat of the scornful. But his delight is in the law of the Lord; and in his law does he meditate day and night." Fixing one's mind on God and His law enables the righteous person to avoid wickedness. Our connection and relationship with Jesus keep our thoughts on Him. It is crucial to begin the day with a meaningful worship, reading the Word of God and praying. As often as possible, we lift our minds to God in thanksgiving, asking for guidance or just praising Him in song, even when we may not sing audibly. This concentration keeps us focused on our Lord and Savior to overcome trials and temptations. By allowing ourselves to have an intimate relationship with God, we experience His power in our lives.

Jesus did not die in vain. His blood is efficacious, which gives us victory over sin. The power that transformed Saul, a murderer, to Paul, a great apostle, is still available. The power that changed Matthew from a deceitful tax collector to a disciple of Jesus still exits. The power of Jesus Christ changes us daily to be like Him. Christ transforms people from sinners into saints. Let us give ourselves entirely to God and allow Him to change us to be like Him. Will you let Christ convert you?

Chapter 9

A Peculiar Life

It is interesting that Scripture calls God's people peculiar. "But ye are a chosen generation, a royal priesthood, an holy nation, a peculiar people; that ye should shew forth the praises of him who hath called you out of darkness into his marvellous light" (1 Peter 2:9 KJV). The *Lexico Dictionary* defines peculiar as "different" from what is "normal or expected."[1] Other dictionaries give a similar definition. Why would God instruct His people to be peculiar? Let the Word of God give us the answers. "Once you were not a people, but now you are the people of God; once you had not received mercy, but now you have received mercy" (1 Peter 2:10, NIV).

We also read, "For the grace of God that brings salvation has appeared to all men, teaching us that denying ungodliness and worldly lust, we should live soberly, righteously, and godly, in the present age, looking for that blessed hope, and the glorious appearing of our great God and Savior Jesus Christ, who gave Himself for us, that he might redeem us from every lawless deed and purify for Himself His own special people, zealous for good works" (Titus 2:11–14). So, Jesus Christ "gave himself that he might redeem us from all iniquity, and purify unto himself a people for his own, zealous for good works." To that end, peculiar refers to God's own people, whom Jesus redeemed at a price beyond measure. The *Seventh-day Bible Commentary*, on the book of Titus, states that every Christian is privately owned by God.[2] God's people are special, as other Bible translations call them. They are different from the rest – in that sense, they are peculiar.

Peculiar People Through the Blood

God's grace, forgiveness, and the indwelling of the Holy Spirit make God's people peculiar. These are people who have surrendered themselves to God so that He can overcome evil for them. These are people who live their lives for God. Whatever they do is meant to bring glory to God. Those who are godly are to turn away from ungodliness and worldliness. That is what makes God's people peculiar or special. Those who do not know God or who have rejected Him and His ways may find God's people unusual, or even abnormal. Come to think of it, who loves one's enemy? Who refuses to do something they feel like doing just because the Bible calls it sin? That sounds very weird to people who do whatever they want, whenever they want.

In the book *Education,* White describes some of the distractions that keep people from dedicating themselves entirely to God to be peculiar. She says, "An intensity such as never before was seen is taking possession of the world. In amusement, in moneymaking, in the contest for power, in the very struggle for existence, there is a terrible force that engrosses body and mind and soul. In the midst of this maddening rush, God is speaking. He bids us come apart and commune with Him. 'Be still, and know that I am God, Psalm46:10.'"[3] It is only God's grace that can enable a human being living in times like these to be still and to let God be in charge.

It is effortless for us to get caught up in the wave of moneymaking and the pursuit of power and pleasure. Undoubtedly, many of us can make use of some extra dollars in our accounts. And while there is nothing wrong with money, obsessive love of it is dreadful. The only way to be safely focused on God is to let Him change us from carnally-minded to Spirit-filled individuals. Then we will be able to overcome the "terrible force that engrosses body and mind and soul." Our minds, our souls, and hearts will be all for Him.

Peculiar people submit to God's law through the power of the Spirit, who lives in them. It is only through the Holy Spirit that God's people can overcome sin and the indulgence that leads to it. Those who surrender themselves to the Lord are enabled to lead victorious Christian lives in this world. Even though they live in the world, they are not of the world. They are different because Christ lives in them.

Does it Matter What Kind of Life We Lead on Earth?

Absolutely. God expects His people to be different from those who reject Him or those who have not yet surrendered their lives to Him. The Word of God states that those who do not allow Christ to make them righteous shall not inherit the kingdom of God: "Do not be deceived. Neither fornicators, nor idolaters, nor adulterers, nor homosexuals, nor sodomites, nor thieves, nor covetous, nor drunkards, nor revilers, nor extortioners will inherit the kingdom of God. And such were some of you. But you were washed, but you were sanctified, but you were justified in the name of the Lord Jesus and by the Spirit of our God" (1 Corinthians 6:9–11). God expects a change of attitude and character in His people.

Justification and sanctification go together. Once we take Jesus as our Savior, we should not continue to live in sin. The Lord calls us to turn away from anything that the Bible calls sin. It is overcoming sin that makes God's people peculiar. And God does not let people figure out what sin is on their own. The Bible tells us exactly what sin is and what should not be practiced by God's people.

God's peculiar people have an attitude of obedience to Him. They purpose to do the revealed will of God, as we have it in the Bible. They pray for the power to do what the Word says. They do not choose to obey some parts of the Bible and ignore others. Moreover, God's people do not change the Word of God to be in line with their desires. They allow God to change them so that they get in line with His Word. In *The Desire of Ages*, White says, "All true obedience comes from the heart. It was heart work with Christ. And if we consent, He will so identify Himself with our thoughts and aims, so blend our hearts and minds into conformity to His will, that when obeying Him, we shall be but carrying out our own impulses. The will, refined and sanctified, will find its highest delight in doing His service."[4] God is gracious. He makes the process of our salvation a delight to those who are willing.

There is, however, a problem when people want to identify with the Lord, yet refuse to allow Him to change them. God is holy, and His people must be holy too. Over and over again, Scripture tells us that God's people must be different. There is much confusion in the world today concerning Christianity. Part of the bewilderment happens because many churchgoers claim to be Christians, but they do not want to lead peculiar lives. Yet Scripture tells us, "Do not love the world or the things in the world. If anyone loves the world, the love of the Father is not in him. For all that is in the world—the lust of the flesh, the lust of the eyes, and the pride of life—is not of the Father but is of the world. And the world is passing away, and the lust of it; but he who does the will of God abides forever" (1 John 2:15–17). The lust of the flesh, the eyes (referring to the natural human desires), and the pride of life, especially when people achieve worldly success, are temptations we face in the world.

The innate evil desires that are contrary to the will of God are the same desires humans faced during the time of Adam and Eve, and when Jesus walked on earth and still today. Those are the three temptations that Satan uses to mislead humankind. But while Adam and Eve succumbed and sinned, Jesus did not sin at all. Instead, He used the Word of God to resist the devil. God gives His people the power to overcome their lusts, but each person must be willing to allow God to work in him or her to overcome. Then and only then will a person become peculiar.

Let's Emulate Jesus

Our Lord, Jesus, is so peculiar that He teaches His followers to love their enemies and to be a blessing to those who curse them. Christ requires Christians to do good things to those who hate them and pray for those who deliberately persecute them. When God's people do good things to those who hate and mistreat them, they show the love of God, who gives life and other blessings to all. It can never get more unusual than that. Rhetorically speaking, who does good to those who hate them?

Jesus was the most peculiar, special, individual who ever walked on earth. Referring to adultery, He taught that lust for a woman in one's heart equals the act itself (Matthew 5:27, 28). He had the power to avoid the painful death on the cross, yet He chose to do the will of God, thus yielded to crucifixion.

The Bible teaches God's children to emulate Christ. And the only way to follow our Savior is to have Him live in us through the Holy Spirit of God. Only then are we able to manifest the fruit of the Holy Spirit: "love, joy, peace, longsuffering, kindness, goodness, faithfulness, gentleness, and self-control" (Galatians 5:22, 23). These are the characteristics of peculiar people. They love God so much that they seek to do His will according to His Word. They love others so much that they use their time to visit and talk to the sick, the lonely, and those who need encouragement. God's peculiar people love others so much that they use their money and other resources to bless those in need. In their lives, they exhibit joy and peace, patience, and faithfulness. These people are kind and gentle. They are meek and very well controlled.

The life of a true Christian manifests all the qualities of the fruit of the Holy Spirit. Yet, they do not come from the individual's own doing but from Christ, who lives in them. With complete surrender to God and prayer for the Holy Spirit to take control, God's people receive power to lead godly lives. God is faithful and able. The Lord will prepare us for His everlasting kingdom if we let Him. Let us allow Him to make each one of us peculiar and sustain us to the end.

Chapter 10

Obedience in Surrender

Surrender is an act of obedience to God. And there is no surrender without compliance. Even within human circles, when two armies fight, there comes a time when one is forced to submit to the other. Usually, the weaker one capitulates and takes orders from the stronger one. Surrendering to God is different in that it comes out of love. God does not force anyone to submit to Him.

People give their hearts to God willingly because they trust in His goodness and faithfulness. That happens in the setting of a loving relationship between the person and God. As we see in the Bible, obedience is crucial for the surrendered people of God. "Since you have purified your souls in obeying the truth through the Spirit in sincere love of the brethren, love one another fervently with a pure heart, having been born again, not of corruptible seed but incorruptible, through the word of God which lives and abides forever" (1 Peter 1:22, 23).

Sin defiles, but when sinners yield to the working of the Holy Spirit, who enables them to obey the truth as we find it in the Bible, their souls get purified. Obedience to the truth does not only cleanse the soul; it also brings about sanctification, the process through which we grow spiritually and are gradually changed to the image of God. Jesus prayed, "Sanctify them by Your truth. Your word is truth" (John17:17). So, it is vital for people to understand the truth about the love of God for them, the death of the Savior, Jesus Christ, and make willful, informed decision to give their lives to God and to obey Him throughout their lives. Dr. Mathew Jennings posits, "True obedience must involve understanding and agreement. The highest level of obedience has its origin in understanding friendship."[1] Also, 2 John 1:6 makes it very clear that God wants His people to obey Him.

Jesus on Obedience

Jesus highlights the importance of obeying His Word. "If you abide in My word, you are My disciples indeed. And you shall know the truth, and the truth shall make you free" (John 8:31, 32). He continues to say, "Anyone who loves me will obey my teaching. My Father will love them, and we will come to them and make our home with them" (John 14:23, NIV). Whoever obeys the Word is a true disciple of Jesus, and God, the Father, and Jesus Christ will come and dwell in the heart of that person, in the form of the Holy Spirit.

When we talk about obedience to God or even the teachings of Jesus, we cannot avoid God's commandments, which the Lord summarized into two: "You shall love the Lord your God with all your heart, with all your soul, and with all your mind. This is the first and great commandment. And the second is like it: 'You shall love your neighbor as yourself.' On these two commandments hang all the law and the prophets" (Matthew 22:37–40). The whole Bible teaches us how to love God and humanity. It also goes on to give us details on how to love. For example, if we love God, we do not worship idols or value anything, whether money, fame, or even life itself, more than God. If we love others, we do not kill them or steal from them. If we love others, we do not practice racism. We do not heap false accusations against them. Loving others, including our enemies, is part of our obedience to God.

I get so encouraged when I realize that God makes it possible for anyone willing to obey Him to do it, in that when a person surrenders totally to Him, the Lord changes the mind and the heart of that individual to be in line with God's will. Ellen White says, "All true obedience comes from the heart... And if we consent, He will so identify Himself with our thoughts and aims, so blend our hearts and minds into conformity to His will, that when obeying Him, we shall be but carrying out our own impulses. The will, refined and sanctified, will find its highest delight in doing His service."[2]

Obedience to God is crucial in our spiritual growth. The more we prayerfully involve our will to do what the Word of God tells us, the easier it becomes for us to obey Him, and the more we get changed to be like God. Dr. Jennings puts it well, "Change of heart occurs when a person makes a willful choice to do what reason and conscience determine is best."[3] That change of heart continues throughout our lives, as long as we willingly obey His voice by His grace.

Obedience Makes a Difference

A story is told about two soldiers who went swimming in the Indian Ocean during working hours. When their commander asked about their whereabouts, he was told that they were swimming at the beach. The commander went after them, and when he spotted them, he shouted, "Come out." But the soldiers ignored him and continued to swim away from the shore. The commander shouted again, "Come out!"

At that point, one of the soldiers turned and started swimming toward the commander. The other soldier continued swimming toward the deep sea. So while one swam away in defiance, the other swam back in obedience. Unfortunately, while the two soldiers continued to swim, a strong storm hit the ocean, and both soldiers drowned. Their bodies were later recovered. And even though they suffered the same fate, they were not treated the same way. The soldier who died while swimming back toward the commander was honored as one who died on duty. The other, who died while swimming away in defiance, received the dishonor of abandoning his responsibility. As a result, the family of the soldier who died after he had obeyed the commander received compensation while the other did not. Obedience made all the difference.

The Bible tells us that we all have gone astray (Isaiah 53:6). We are all sinners who need God's forgiveness and redemption. Jesus came down and paid the penalty for our sins. The difference between those who will be saved and those who will be lost is the response of each person to the Lord's invitation to accept God's forgiveness, restoration, and life.

There is a big difference between someone who disobeys God and lives in sin and another who obeys and gives his life to God. Those who reject God have no regard for Him or His Word. But those who surrender themselves to God allow Christ to enable them to live godly lives. A surrendered person has a deep hatred for sin because the grace of God puts enmity between the person and sin. Part of the fruit of the Holy Spirit is love for God and others, which gives an intense passion for doing the will of God to those who surrender to Him. And our relationship with God—our surrender and love for Him—is reflected in our obedience to His Word.

Jesus said that our righteousness should exceed that of the Pharisees and scribes. Pharisees had a perfect outward show of piety. They had many rules for people to follow that they themselves did not observe. So much is said about the Pharisees, but the bottom line is that they were all talk with no action. We need to obey God by His grace. “Not by might nor power, but by my Spirit” (Zechariah 4:6). Will you surrender yourself fully to God?

Chapter 11

Trusting God With Your Life

The Bible presents us with people in various situations of life. While some seem to have led comfortable lives, others faced incredible difficulties, enough to have caused them fear and despair. Yet, they trusted God with their lives. It is very encouraging that none of those who trusted God with their lives got disappointed. For instance, David, the psalmist, had many enemies who were out to take his life. Day and night, David's enemies sought ways to kill him. And he was well aware of his situation.

He said, "For I hear the slander of many; Fear is on every side; While they take counsel together against me, They scheme to take away my life. But as for me, I trust in You, O LORD; I say, 'You are my God.' My times are in Your hand; Deliver me from the hand of my enemies, And from those who persecute me" (Psalm 31:13–15). Since David put his trust in the hands of the Almighty God, he was protected. Hence, David was able to subdue all his enemies. His prayer, "Let me not be ashamed, O Lord," was answered.

What about Mary, the mother of Jesus? When God sent the angel Gabriel to tell her that she would be the Savior's mother, Mary was already engaged to Joseph. The message of God through the angel could have raised many questions in Mary. *Will this affect my engagement to Joseph? Do I qualify to take the responsibility of being the mother of the Savior? What if I reject God's plan and go on with my marriage plans?* But look at Mary's response after the angel explained God's plan for her: “Then Mary said, ‘Behold the maidservant of the Lord! Let it be to me according to your word.’ And the angel departed from her” (Luke 1:38). Mary trusted God; she surrendered to the will of God.

And look how faithful God is to those who trust Him. When Joseph realized that Mary was expectant, he contemplated leaving her. But God intervened. The angel of the Lord appeared to Joseph and assured him that God had chosen Mary to be the mother of the Savior and that the pregnancy was the work of the Holy Spirit. The angel encouraged Joseph to go ahead and marry Mary as planned.

“When Joseph woke up, he did what the angel of the Lord had commanded him and took Mary home as his wife. But he did not consummate their marriage until she gave birth to a son. And he gave him the name Jesus” (Matthew 1:24, 25). Mary trusted God with her life, and God took care of her.

Does God intervene and provide for the needs of His people today? Absolutely. My experience with the Lord is that He can faithfully take care of His people more than we can ever imagine. Before I learned that, I often experienced high levels of stress, not because I had no food to eat or a place to sleep, but because I was anxious about “tomorrow.” However, as I continued to grow spiritually, I learned that whenever I surrendered my needs to God, He always took care of me and provided for me in ways I could never imagine.

Immediately after I arrived in the United States, I lived in Tennessee, where I taught at-risk teen boys at a home learning center. I did not have a car, and most of the time, I had more financial needs than the money I earned per month. By that time, our family was separated by distance and scattered on two continents. The children were in Africa, David was in Texas, and I was in Calhoun, Tennessee. At the same time, I was going through a culture shock, and I was also stressed by the separation of my family, besides earning very little money from the self-supporting ministry.

To make matters worse, I fell sick during that time, and a doctor put me on some medication that ran out, and the prescription expired before I got well. So, I decided to go back to the doctor's office. I booked an appointment, but I had no transport to the hospital or funds to cover the medical costs. The only money I had was for the consultation fee. I did not have insurance at the time. I recall telling God, "I don't want to miss this doctor's appointment, but I neither have the transportation nor the money for medication. Lord, please organize this trip for me. In Jesus' name, I pray. Amen."

Blessing in Disguise

After I said that prayer, I told myself not to stress about the state of affairs. I decided to wait and see what the Lord would do about the hopeless situation. My appointment was at 4:00 p.m., and from morning until that afternoon, I continued with my work. I made my request to God in the morning without any idea how I was going to get to the doctor's office or where I would get money to pay for the medicine. All I knew was that I was under pressure to seek treatment. As it was getting closer to my appointment time, I thought about canceling the appointment. But at 3:00 p.m., a colleague knocked on my office door and walked in, asking how I was doing. I took the opportunity to explain to him the situation concerning my appointment.

"I don't quite understand how I am doing right now. I think I am troubled," I said.

"When is the appointment?" he asked. I told him that it was in an hour.

"I'll take you there," he said.

Later, as we drove off from the parking lot, he remembered that he had first to pick up something from the staff apartments, quite a distance away though still on campus. On our way out, another colleague stopped us for a minute or two. As if this was not enough, we stopped to put gas in the car. When I set our time for departure, I did not expect those delays. By the time we arrived at the doctor's office, it was already too late for the doctor to see me. I was told to reschedule my appointment. But before I did, I requested to talk to the nurse who usually assisted the doctor.

When I explained my problem to the nurse, she decided to give me some free samples of the medication that I needed. She gave me enough to last one month when I would go back to see the doctor. And since I did not see the doctor, I did not pay the consultation fee. God solved my problems. From this experience, I learned that I should take every problem—big or small—to God. I have remembered this experience many times, especially when I find myself in a dilemma.

Nothing Puzzles God

We all have needs, regardless of who we are. While some need healing, others need to maintain good health. While some need wisdom and knowledge to manage their wealth to last their lifetime and beyond, others require the grace to put food on their tables every day. Some people need to change their immigration status. Many students and immigrants who came to the United States to get an education or pursue the "American Dream" find themselves struggling very hard to make ends meet. Many times, their visas expire before they attain their dreams. Then they have to make the tough decision of either going back to their country without the education they came for or struggling to survive in America.

Many choose to stay in America. As a result, they end up working illegally, and mostly, working underpaying jobs. This situation has thrown many men and women into despair. Some of those who have been in America for long prefer not to return to their home countries because they consider it a waste of time and other resources to go back before they achieve what brought them to America in the first place.

You often hear someone say something similar to this: "After all the years I have hassled in America, what do I have to show for it? Think about the opportunity cost. Had I stayed in my country, I could have had a degree by now, or a good business. And most likely, I would have a family, too. How can I go back home emptyhanded after these ten and more years?" Others choose to overstay their visas because they have nothing to fall back on in their own countries. That is a cause of stress for many people.

Others, even though they are legal or permanent residents of America or are American citizens, have their share of problems. Some are either unemployed or underemployed. Others are hurting from separation, divorce, terminal illness or drug addiction, and their loved ones. There are problems everywhere in the world. While some are common to humans, regardless of location, others exist uniquely in particular parts of the world. No matter where you live on earth, and no matter the situation in your life, if you surrender yourself to God and put every aspect of your life in His hands, He will give you the wisdom to sort things out and guide you as you organize your life by making the right decisions.

Ellen White states, "When in trouble, we too often go for help to our brethren, who are no wiser nor stronger than ourselves; but if we would go to Jesus, if we would take our troubles to Him in prayer, we should find rest, and peace, and courage. The wisdom that God gives is unerring; His strength is sufficient for all our needs."[1] Whatever your needs, "Seek first the kingdom of God and His righteousness, and all these things shall be added to you" (Matthew 6:33). The Lord has the power to help each one of us, regardless of our circumstances. We just need to trust Him with our lives.

Seek God's Kingdom and Righteousness

The call for us to put God first in our lives is a call for us to set our priorities right. The Lord wants us to realize that eternal life is more important than anything else of value on earth. Unless we love God, it is not possible to let Him be first in our lives. If we love God with all our hearts, minds, and souls, it means we love Him intimately. Then we will meditate upon Him and do whatever He instructs us to do, by His grace. Our love for God and our intimate relationship with Him will compel us to love others dearly, which calls for a deep connection with the Lord. It is in that kind of a relationship with our heavenly Father that we can trust Him with our lives.

When Jesus lived on earth, He surrendered to the Father's will, and He was able to trust God and to put Him first in His life. If you study Jesus' prayer life in the Bible, you will realize that He was always in touch with His Father. The connection and relationship between the two enabled Jesus to pray, "O My Father, if this cup cannot pass away from Me unless I drink it, Your will be done" (Matthew 26:42). That level of surrender portrays Christ's trust in God.

As followers of Christ, we need to trust God and establish a sincere, loving relationship with Him. Our relationship with the Lord will enable us to make the kingdom of God and His righteousness a priority in our lives. God is faithful. He will provide for all our spiritual, physical, mental, social, and emotional needs, according to His will. Will you trust your life with God?

Chapter 12

Leaning on God

"Abide in Me, and I in you. As the branch cannot bear fruit of itself, unless it abides in the vine, neither can you, unless you abide in Me" (John 15:4). Unless we get firmly connected to Christ, we cannot bear any spiritual fruit. When a branch is detached from the vine, it withers and dies. Likewise, we spiritually die when we get disconnected from God. Let me explain this point. Whenever I am reading a book in a room with dim lighting, I use a portable light stand that I connect to the nearest socket. As long as the power cord for my lamp is connected to the outlet, I have adequate lighting on my study table and book. But when I unplug the cable from the socket, the light disappears. That is not surprising because the light stand can only give light if its cord is inside the power source. Also, I once had a computer that the battery would only turn on and retain power if the cable was plugged into the socket.

Christians are like that portable light stand. They are also like the computer that could not turn on unless the cord was plugged into the power source. People can only thrive spiritually and serve the Lord genuinely if they are in the Lord. In John 15:1–8, Christ emphasizes the importance of staying connected to Him, allowing the Savior to dwell in the heart perpetually. As Ellen White says, "A close connection with heaven will give the right tone to your fidelity and will be the ground of your success."[1] It is through the connection with the Savior that Christians gain victory over evil. Then, they can serve God faithfully and enjoy the blessings of their salvation.

Human Power in Spiritual Matters

When Moses presented God's laws to the children of Israel, with confidence, they promised to do everything the Lord required:

> So Moses came and told the people all the words of the LORD and all the judgments. And all the people answered with one voice and said, "All the words which the LORD has said we will do"... Then he took the Book of the Covenant and read in the hearing of the people. And they said, "All that the LORD has said we will do, and be obedient." And Moses took the blood, sprinkled it on the people, and said, "This is the blood of the covenant which the LORD has made with you according to all these words." (Exodus 24:3, 7, 8)

No sooner did the Israelites promise to obey God than they built a golden calf and worshipped it. However, Moses knew better than keeping his trust in human strength or wisdom. While the Israelites talked with much confidence in themselves, Moses told God, "If Your Presence does not go with us, do not bring us up from here" (Exodus 33:15). Moses had learned that without God's presence among the Israelites, they could not survive. As long as God was on their side, not even the Red Sea could thwart the journey to the promised land. Water streamed from the rock in the desert, a cloud shielded them from the sun, and a pillar of fire lighted the way at night. As long as God was with the Israelites, no nation ever defeated them. Moses knew that on his own, he had no power to perform those miracles. He rightly understood that he was just an instrument through which God Himself led the Israelites and provided for their needs.

In our spiritual walk and our life on earth, we face many obstacles because of sin. Many situations in this life, such as divorce, depression, sickness, poverty, addiction to overeating, drugs, or other things, frustrate people, even to the point of death. Our merciful God is ready to help those who will let Him.

Jesus calls all who are overburdened to go to Him. The Savior wants us to give Him all our problems. But if we solve them without Him, we may get a temporary relief instead of a permanent solution. Jesus Himself is the solution. In *The Desire of Ages,* White states, "Those who take Christ at His word, and surrender their souls to His keeping, their lives to His ordering, will find peace and quietude…Our lives may seem a tangle; but as we commit ourselves to the wise Master-worker, He will bring out the pattern of life and character that will be to His own glory."[2]

We need the power to love and do good to those who hate us and do evil things to us. We need grace to forgive those who deliberately hurt us. Also, it is God's grace that makes it possible for us to leave judgment to God. Our wisdom and power will fail us in spreading the gospel of Jesus Christ. We must rely on the Lord for us to succeed in our spiritual walk.

One of the most encouraging things about our relationship with God is that, as long as we give ourselves to Him, He takes over and leads the way. Scripture tells us to trust in the Lord only, not in our human power or wisdom (Proverbs 3:5,6). Pray for the grace to surrender yourself and all your needs to God.

God's Faithfulness

A story is told about God's faithfulness to a young boy. A group of teenage girls went to the woods in a village in Kenya to get firewood. Each girl took a machete for cutting dry branches and a rope to tie their firewood, and off they went, talking, joking, and laughing. After walking some distance through tall grass and thick bushes, they realized that one of the girls' younger brother was following them. “Why are you following us? Go back home,” said the sister. The boy stood still, but when the girls resumed walking, he, too, started and continued following them, a few footsteps behind.

“Go back. We are going far, and you will be exhausted,” the sister instructed.

“I want to come and get firewood. Look, I have a rope to tie my firewood,” said the boy. In vain, the girls tried all they could to convince the boy to go back. Eventually, they let him trail them as they walked through the forest, cutting dry tree branches for firewood. Their mission took them deep into the woods. After some time, the boy caught up with the girls, and he, too, started collecting firewood. Suddenly, while they were preoccupied with their work, a rhino appeared from a distance. In a split second, the girls took to their heels, running as fast as they could.

In their panic, they forgot about the boy. The poor lad ran too, but he could not keep up with the girls. Within a few minutes, the young women were out of sight. All that the boy could see were bushes, tall trees, and an endless mass of thick, tall grass. But as he ran, he remembered something he learned at church. His teacher had taught him that Jesus never leaves His children and that when in trouble, one should call on Him for help.

The boy started saying, “Jesus, please, stay with me; Jesus, please, don't leave me.” After running for some time, he looked back and could not see the rhino anymore. By that time, he was too tired to keep running. He walked as fast as he could, going toward the direction of his home. As for the girls, they ran until they reached the home of one of their friends. As some of them started to narrate their experience in the forest, the boy's sister remembered her brother and burst out crying. Several adults took all the weapons they could lay their hands on and left for the woods to look for the boy. They did not go very far before they ran into him. Nonetheless, they were surprised to see the boy walking, though looking tired and scared, but otherwise OK.

"I asked Jesus to remain with me. Then when I was too tired to run anymore, I looked back and did not see the rhino," said the boy. Even those who had never considered Christianity wanted to know more about Jesus that day. God wants to be with us in all situations of our lives.

There are times I feel like nobody understands what I am going through. Then my eyes of faith look up, and I pray, "God, I thank you that I do not need to tell you anything about my situation. You know me better than I know myself. Please, Lord, help me."

God is faithful. He promises to stay with us, to lead us and to save us. "He who has begun a good work in you will complete it until the day of Jesus Christ" (Philippians 1:6). Trust the Lord wholeheartedly and lean on Him. You will never be disappointed. Let us lean on Jesus for all our needs.

Chapter 13

Heeding the Commission

Some experiences are so compelling that once people go through them, they never remain the same. And while some of them change people for the worse, others leave people better than ever before. Of all the occurrences, encountering Jesus Christ is the best and most powerful; it makes one a new creature, filled with the hope of eternal life. For that reason, Christ being the loving Savior that He is, sent His disciples to spread the gospel to the whole world. He told them, "Go therefore and make disciples of all the nations, baptizing them in the name of the Father and of the Son and of the Holy Spirit, teaching them to observe all things that I have commanded you; and lo, I am with you always, even to the end of the age" (Matthew 28:19, 20). Every surrendered Christian should heed that commission under the Holy Spirit's guidance and follow in the footsteps of the Savior.

Ellen White explains the Lord's commission very well. She says, "Love for souls for whom Christ died means crucifixion of self. He who is a child of God should henceforth look upon himself as a link in the chain let down to save the world, one with Christ in His plan of mercy, going forth with Him to seek and save the lost. The Christian is ever to realize that he has consecrated himself to God and that in character, he is to reveal Christ to the world. The self-sacrifice, the sympathy, the love, manifested in the life of Christ are to reappear in the life of the worker for God."[1]

Christians are called to witness and teach others about the Word of God. The goal is to make disciples for Jesus Christ by revealing the love of God and the offer of eternal life through the Savior. People need to see the love and compassion of Jesus in those who spread the Word to the world. We are all commissioned to witness and to point others to the Lord. But we have many obstacles, real and imaginary.

Beyond our Comfort Zones

Several years ago, I attended a two-week seminar at the church in Bowman Hills, Tennessee. One evening, the pastor led a discussion about why people fear to ask God to send them anywhere in the world to witness for Him. He encouraged people to share their thoughts. "Very often, I hear people say that they hesitate to ask God to send them anywhere He pleases because they do not want the Lord to send them to some places. What are your fears? Let's discuss them today," he said.

Several people spoke and shared the reasons why they did not ask God to send them wherever He pleased. The majority of the people feared the unknown. They were unsure what would happen if they surrendered to do God's will and allowed Him to do whatever He deemed fit with them. But others knew precisely why they did not ask God to send them wherever He wanted. They feared that God would send them to places where they did not want to go.

Then I said to myself, *I have traveled from one continent to another. I was born and brought up in Africa, in one of the low-income families, and one of the poorest districts in Kenya. Why wouldn't I ask God to send me wherever He pleased?* It was then that I remembered my childhood days when I came home from school and found my mother outside our hut in the village. She would say to me, "Please, take off your school uniform, put on your work clothes, and run to the river for water. Here, take this gourd and rope, and tie your gourd quickly and go. You don't want the sun to set before you get back home. Walking in the darkness is dangerous with all the deadly cobras and puff adders around."

Often, my answer went like this: "Yes, Mother! If you see any of my friends going to the river, please, tell them to wait for me." I would tell Mother this as I disappeared into the hut to change my clothes before I started trekking the eight or so miles to the river, where I would fill my gourd with water and carry it on my back with the help of the rope across my head.

Mother would say something like, "Hurry up! If anybody is going for water now, you will meet them on the way. I am not staying home either. I am taking a machete and a rope to the forest to cut firewood from a dry tree branch that I saw yesterday. Otherwise, we will be in total darkness tonight. Not even one piece of firewood is left to light the hut tonight, let alone for cooking supper."

As my childhood life flashed through my mind, sitting in church that evening, I thought, *With my background, where in the world, can't I go? I am used to drought, famine, and life in the woods. For many years I lived in a hut without running water or electricity. I lived my life for many years without vehicles, telephones, radios, or televisions. I saw wild animals, such as buffalos and rhinos, walking freely in my father's property. Many times I heard of neighbors who were trampled to death. Two of my cousins died from snakebites. My elder sister and two of my younger siblings died from diseases such as measles. I saw witch doctors in the village welding incredible power. Yet the witch doctors who treated people to prevent them from witchcraft and death succumbed to death themselves. God saved me from that environment and showed me His love and power in sustaining His own. Where in the world can't I go to serve the Lord? Why should I fear to ask God to send me wherever He wants?*

Then I realized that I, too, had my fears. Even in Kenya, where I lived for decades, there were many locations I never visited, and other regions I considered worse than my drought-stricken home district. There were places I feared to go, too. Ellen White states, "Many who profess to be Christ's followers have an anxious, troubled heart because they are afraid to trust themselves with God. They do not make a complete surrender to Him, for they shrink from the consequences that such a surrender may involve. Unless they do make this surrender, they cannot find peace."[2] What a life to live as a Christian!

Wherever God will send us to work for Him, He will lead the way, and He will be with us all the time. Those who put Paul and Silas in jail could not prevent the Lord from staying with His servants. Paul and Silas sang and prayed until the prison shook. The doors opened, and the chains dropped from them. As a result, the jailer and his family got converted.

When we encounter the Savior and surrender our lives totally to Him, nothing will hold us from sharing the good news. A good example is the Samaritan woman who met Jesus at the well. "The woman then left her waterpot, went her way into the city, and said to the men, 'Come, see a Man who told me all things that I ever did. Could this be the Christ?' Then they went out of the city and came to Him" (John 4:28–30). It is incredible how this woman met Jesus at the well. After a conversation that began by Jesus asking her for water to drink, the woman left her waterpot to pursue a more important mission than fetching literal water. "And many of the Samaritans of that city believed on Him for the saying of the woman, which testified, He told me all that I ever did" (John 4:39). God does not expect us to convert people. Conversion of hearts is the work of the Holy Spirit. But the Lord calls us to tell others about our experiences as Christians and to teach them His Word.

Christ wants His followers to go out of their way to witness for Him. "Make disciples of the nations," said Jesus. God demonstrated His desire to save everybody by sending His Son to die for every human being. He knows the hope, peace, and joy people receive when they accept Jesus as their Savior and Lord. God becomes their Father, and He wants the same for everyone.

God instructs His people to love Him and to love other people. If we love God, we will seek to please Him by doing His will, including pointing others to the Savior for eternal life. And our efforts will not go to waste because Jesus did not die in vain. There is power in His blood to save.

Seize Opportunities

We do not have unlimited time to witness to others about Christ. Our chances are limited by many circumstances, including death. Missing an opportunity to introduce a person to Christ leaves a terrible memory when the person dies before ever turning to the Savior. David and I had a scary experience involving one of our neighbors—an adult woman who lived with her mother. One afternoon, David came to the apartment where we lived and told me, "I just met our neighbor's daughter walking toward the front gate, and she asked me to call the police for her."

"What for?" I asked.

"She did not explain. She just whispered quickly and told me that her friend's boyfriend has come for her at gunpoint. The guy wants our neighbor to drive him to a place, but our neighbor thinks she may not come back. She has told me that the guy has drugs and an illegal gun," explained David.

"Where was the guy when our neighbor's daughter whispered that to you," I asked.

Strangely, the guy was in the lady's car outside the gate. David did not even see the guy, and before David could ask our neighbor any more questions, she hurried away to the waiting car. Nonetheless, David called the police immediately and explained everything he heard from the lady.

By the time the police arrived, the young lady and the man were out of sight. We hoped that the police would catch up with them before it was too late. The incident impacted me so much because, for months, I had intended to introduce the lady to Jesus. Regardless of my desire to point her to the Savior, I did not know how to go about it. I was relatively new in the United States, and differences in our cultures and lifestyle made it so difficult for me to get familiar with her enough to talk about the Lord. A few weeks before the incident, she and I had an opportunity to talk about Christianity. After that, I became more confident to speak to her about salvation matters, but I was not in a hurry to pursue her for Christ. *She is my neighbor,* I thought. *I will talk to her whenever time offers itself.*

Now she had been driven away at gunpoint, fearing for her life. I wished I had been more proactive in introducing her to the Lord. Then I prayed, "God, please give me a second chance to tell our neighbor about You. Please, protect her and bring her back home safely. Lead the young man to know You too. In Jesus' name, I pray. Amen."

Immediately after I finished praying, I heard a loud knock on our door, and on opening, the mother of the young lady who had been taken away stood there. "I just came back to find my daughter missing in the apartment. As I wondered about what had happened, a policeman came and told me that somebody took her away at gunpoint," she said.

“Do you have any idea who the man could be?” I asked.

“I don't know him, but he has been calling our landline and threatening to kill both my daughter and me,” she replied.

“Why?” I asked.

“I don’t know,” she said and kept quiet. I sensed that she did not want to say much. So I stopped asking her any more questions about the issue. Then she gave me a small piece of paper with a telephone number on it. “This is my cell phone number. Could you, please, keep it and call me if you see anything?” she requested.

I took the paper and asked her whether we could pray together. She gave her consent. I prayed for her and her daughter. I asked God to save the lives of both the young lady and the man who had taken her away. When we opened our eyes, the mother thanked me profoundly. I was glad that she agreed to pray with me. Then she left.

A day later, the mother told us that her daughter and the man were in police custody. After two more days, the young lady came home. This time I extended myself to pray for her. She was not in the right mood to do that at the time, nonetheless. She, however, promised to come to my apartment later, which she did.

We talked for some time about her health condition. Even though she was barely sober, I decided to go ahead and introduce her to Jesus. I told her that our family had been praying for her. Then she said, “Oh, thank you very much for praying for me. The guy who took me is my girlfriend's boyfriend, and he wanted to use my car to deliver marijuana to his customers. He drove my car to a place that fits the description of hell. I have never been so scared in my life. But after all that mess, the police found us and took us to jail. I called my friend, who is a lawyer, and he came and got me out.”

The guy who took her at gunpoint was still in jail. I prayed to God to save him. I told her that I was glad that she was out and that

Jesus loved her and would like to save her and give her peace. As I was just starting to talk to her about Jesus, her phone rang, and she stood up to go. It was her boyfriend coming to see her. As she was about to leave, I gave her the book *Steps to Christ* by Ellen White. "This book is very nice. I recommend it to you. It talks about Jesus, the Savior, who loves you and would like to save you if you accept Him. He will give you peace in your life. Could you please read it, and next time we meet, tell me what you think about it?" I requested. She took the book, and before I could say much, her cell phone rang again. It was her boyfriend still, and she had to go.

A few days later, the mother and her daughter relocated before I had a chance to follow up with the young lady. However, I continued to pray that God would save them. Later, after we bought a house and moved from that neighborhood, I thought that God had kept us at the apartment to teach the mother and daughter and others about Him. However, I felt as if I had not done much for the Lord. What could I have done differently to reach more people for Christ?

Chapter 14

Influencing Others for Christ

As a student in a Leadership and School Administration program, one of my favorite courses was Ethical Leadership. And one of the assignments in the class asked, "How can you influence a person, a group, or an organization to do better ethics or morality?" The professor who taught the course instructed us to discuss how we influenced someone poorly, as well as how we did it well in the past and our plans to do it right in the future.

In the process of contemplating my past successes and failures, and plans to improve my future performance, in influencing others to do better ethics, I remembered my experience as a missionary teacher in one of the schools where I taught. I will just refer to it as a learning center. Even though I had been a teacher and a school administrator before, my experience at my new school was different from my previous ones. The students at this school challenged everything I knew about teaching, school administration, and leadership in that while my former students wanted to be in school, despite breaking school rules, these boys did anything possible to instigate their expulsion from the center. Thus, the center turned out to be the most challenging place to achieve any educational goals, whether spiritual, mental, physical, emotional, or social.

I quickly embraced the reality that at the center, I taught at-risk teen boys who had been expelled from other schools due to various issues. Police had to escort some of the boys to the center because their parents could not handle them. The program at that learning center was set up to help those kinds of students. Some of the intervention and treatment measures included having the boys to work with their hands, stay away from the television and radio, and to hold them accountable. These were the very things that most of the students disliked the most at the center. They did not want to be held responsible for anything. A good number of them came from home environments without structure. They also did not care much about work ethics. So many of them disliked working, especially doing physical work.

Since these students did not like to be in the program, including the school, they broke the rules on purpose. It took months before the teachers, and other staff could convince them that they needed the program. Before we earned their cooperation, the boys did anything to push the school administration to send them away for good. But contrary to their expectations, we showed them the love of Christ while holding them accountable. We made use of guidance and counseling and encouraged them to stay in the program until they graduated.

In my earlier teaching and leadership duties, I was used to following policies and school rules, until I met these students who devised ways to get out of school forever. And there I was, new in America, experiencing culture shock and dealing with quite a unique experience in my teaching career. How could I influence the boys to like school? How could I impact them for Christ? I realized that policies and school rules alone would never affect the students for education, let alone for Christ.

Love, Acceptance, and Relationship

A few months into my interaction with the at-risk teen boys, I realized that the only thing that seemed to grab their attention, regardless of their behavioral or health issues, was love and acceptance. As long as a student knew that a teacher or staff member cared about him, he paid attention. He listened and tried to follow instructions. This learning center was the turning point of my Christian experience and teaching career. Often, students who were thought to be too depressed or were overcome by other issues, cooperated with teachers because they believed us when we told them that we wanted to help them. They also listened when we told them that Jesus loved them, and He wanted to help them.

I realized that without a relationship, I could neither teach nor witness to the students. But above all, I realized that I had to pray earnestly for the Holy Spirit to guide me and prevail in class for a lesson to end without a student punching another student or running out through the back door. So, to succeed in teaching and witnessing, I needed a relationship with God and the people I needed to witness Christ. I learned a similar lesson in church leadership: People need more than Bible facts. If they don't trust you, they won't believe your message. Regardless of your position in the church, how can you influence others for Christ?

How did Jesus do it?

Jesus interacted with people, sympathized with them, helped them with their needs, and preached to them. His ministry on earth demonstrated the process of reaching people for the kingdom of God. Christ's method encompassed, among other things, selfless love, sympathy, and a deep desire for the lost. White gives us a vivid description of how Jesus went about teaching others for the kingdom. She says, "He reached the hearts of people by going among them as one who desired their good. He sought them in the public streets, in private houses, on the boats, in the synagogue, by the shores of the lake, and at the marriage feast. He met them at their daily vocations, and manifested an interest in their secular affairs…In order to reach all classes, we must meet them where they are."[1] I know that it is possible to live with neighbors for years without even knowing their names. But if we want to witness to others about Jesus, we have to be purposeful, mingle, and interact with them enough to let them give us the chance to share our faith.

Without love, compassion, and a deep desire for others to get saved, it is not possible to get out of our busy schedules to socialize with people for the sake of talking to them about the Savior. But that is the path Jesus paved for us. He sympathized with outcasts such as lepers, prostitutes, and thieves. That is how Mary Magdalene, who was caught in the act of adultery, was forgiven. After she learned about the love of God, she gave her life to Him. Mathew, the tax collector, was disdained because tax collectors did not have the best reputation, especially concerning corruption. But Jesus went to his house and socialized with him and other sinners (Matthew 9:9–12).

"Therefore, as the elect of God, holy and beloved, put on tender mercies, kindness, humility, meekness, longsuffering; bearing with one another, and forgiving one another, if anyone has a complaint against another; even as Christ forgave you, so you also must do" (Colossians 3:12, 13). We need these traits to reach others for Christ, for that is what we are all called to do for our Lord. Our personalities and our cultures dictate much about how we spread the gospel. Some people find it easy to approach others and talk about their faith. Others struggle to greet strangers. Regardless of our personalities, gifts, or talents, if we are willing to witness for God, the Lord will make ways for us to reach the people He wants us to influence to His glory. As long as we are willing, God will work it out for each one of us. Let us pray and ask God to lead us to serve Him according to His will.

We need a loving relationship with God for us to be able to point others to the Savior. If possible, we should establish relationships with the people we need to reach for Christ. I pray that we will emulate Jesus and depend on God in our mission of leading others to Him. Will you allow Jesus to work through you for the salvation of others?

Chapter 15

God Prepares His Workers

The lives of many Bible characters attest to God's diligence in preparing His people for service. Most of the people that God called to His work went through rigorous "training experiences" that got them ready for the job. Ellen White says,

> God takes men as they are, and educates them for His service, if they will yield themselves to Him. The Spirit of God, received into the soul, will quicken all its faculties. Under the guidance of the Holy Spirit, the mind that is devoted unreservedly to God develops harmoniously, and is strengthened to comprehend and fulfill the requirements of God… He who longs to be of service to Christ is so quickened by the life-giving power of the Sun of Righteousness that he is enabled to bear much fruit to the glory of God.[1]

Let us look at some examples of God's servants.

God Prepared Joseph

In chapter seven, we read a bit of Joseph's life story concerning his willingness to let God's will be done in him. Looking at his entire life, we can tell that God was working in him. It was not by chance that Pharaoh said to Joseph, "'You shall be over my house, and all my people shall be ruled according to your word; only in regard to the throne will I be greater than you.' And Pharaoh said to Joseph,

'See, I have set you over all the land of Egypt'" (Genesis 41:40, 41). Think about Joseph's life up to the point when Pharaoh made him the prime minister of Egypt. The significant events in Joseph's life, including Jacob's great love for him, his brothers' hatred toward him, his slavery in Potiphar's house, and the circumstances that led him to prison, all contributed in preparing Joseph for service. Consider Joseph's ability to interpret dreams, which paved the way for him to be a part of Pharaoh's kingdom. God's designed purpose for Joseph's life worked out perfectly well. "All things work together for good to those who love God, to those who are the called according to His purpose" (Romans 8:28). Both the good and bad help to shape God's people spiritually.

Right from a young age, God used dreams to show Joseph his future. People who receive meaningful dreams can relate to that experience. For Joseph, the dreams came to pass after many twists and turn in his life. A lot had happened between the time he had the dreams and the time they came to pass, of which he had no prior knowledge.

Joseph went through "fire" to prepare him for the high position that God had designed for him, and, through it all, God never forgot him. As a slave in Potiphar's house, the Lord gave Joseph favor in the eyes of his master. Think of the big picture. God knew that He would allow His people, the children of Israel, to go to Egypt to save them from starvation. Joseph was the one chosen by God through whom God's people would stay in Egypt.

Joseph's experiences, including his learning at home, up to the time when he got promoted to power, prepared him for service in the high position. His high level of integrity and loyalty is apparent, especially in his interaction with Potiphar's wife. He had learned to honor God, and the Lord remained faithful to Joseph throughout his life. "The LORD was with Joseph, and he was a successful man; and he was in the house of his master the Egyptian. And his master saw that the LORD was with him and that the LORD made all he did to prosper in his hand" (Genesis 39:2, 3). Also, it was God who gave Joseph the wisdom to interpret the dreams of his inmates and later Pharaoh's dreams.

In the end, Joseph told his brothers, "And God sent me before you to preserve a posterity for you in the earth, and to save your lives by a great deliverance" (Genesis 45:7). Later, he also told them, "But as for you, you meant evil against me; but God meant it for good, in order to bring it about as it is this day, to save many people alive" (Genesis 50:20). It is incredible the way God used all these events to get Joseph ready for the excellent service.

By the grace of God, through his endurance, Joseph got ready for his assignment. Remember the spiritual maturity he manifested to his brothers when they found him in Egypt. His attitude toward his brothers and God portrays a spiritual maturity that is only achievable through total surrender to God. Scripture shows us that Joseph carried out his responsibilities exceptionally and successfully (Genesis 41:53, 54). His training worked very well.

God Prepared Moses

God prepared Moses for leadership. Whatever Moses learned in Pharaoh's palace was not enough to qualify him to lead God's people. Hence, Moses was a shepherd for 40 years in the desert. By the time God sent him to lead His people from Egypt to Canaan, he had learned enough patience and endurance to carry out God's assigned duties successfully. By the end of the 40 years in the wilderness, he had learned to humble himself to God.

Remember, Pharaoh's daughter adopted Moses a few months after birth. Can you imagine any king's son or grandson looking after sheep in the wilderness for 40 years? Moses needed the training that he got in the desert because he needed different leadership skills from what he had learned in Pharaoh's palace. He needed to learn to do the will of God instead of his own. How else could Moses teach the stubborn Israelites that God put under his leadership? Scripture's account on Moses' leadership shows that he led the children of Israel through many miracles made possible by the Lord (Exodus 14).

Moses maintained a very close relationship with God throughout his leadership. He had learned to rely on God to succeed in his duties, unlike before, when he took matters into his own hands and killed an Egyptian. From his training, he learned that only God had the power to save and sustain His people. As a result, Moses told God, “If Your Presence does not go with us, do not bring us up from here. For how then will it be known that Your people and I have found grace in Your sight, except You go with us? So we shall be separate, Your people and I, from all the people who are upon the face of the earth” (Exodus 33:15, 16). Any Christian who does not learn the importance of God's presence in one's life and ministry is not worthy of the name. Indeed, God succeeded in training Moses for service.

Does God Prepare People for His Work Anymore?

Absolutely. When God puts a desire in a person to serve Him, He provides all the necessary tools, including a conducive environment for learning and a means to render service. When we have the desire to serve God but feel inadequate, it is not necessarily bad, and it should not prevent us from serving the Lord. Instead, it should lead us to pray for wisdom and knowledge. We should also get out of our way to learn whatever we need to serve according to our calling.

White states, “You may feel the deficiency of your character and the smallness of your ability in comparison with the greatness of the work. But if you had the greatest intellect ever given to man, it would not be sufficient for your work. 'Without Me ye can do nothing,' says our Lord and Saviour. John 15:5. The result of all we do rests in the hands of God."[2] May we always remember that in God's work, we should have confidence in the Lord alone. The work of salvation is God's, in which He has invited us to participate. Therefore, we should always let Him lead because He knows best how to do it, and He alone has the power to make it a success.

The Role of the Holy Spirit in Preparing People for Service

The Holy Spirit performs many duties to prepare people for service. For example, He convicts people of sin, leading them to repentance. He teaches about God by enabling people to understand the Word. He gives people spiritual gifts that allow them to serve God in various ways. Different people are given different gifts according to the kind of service or work the Lord wants each individual to do for Him. "And He Himself gave some to be apostles, some prophets, some evangelists, and some pastors and teachers, for the equipping of the saints for the work of ministry, for the edifying of the body of Christ" (Ephesians 4:11, 12). "Each of you should use whatever gift you have received to serve others, as faithful stewards of God's grace in its various forms" (1 Peter 4:10, NIV). The Holy Spirit equips us with the tools with which to serve. May we always remain humble as we serve through our various gifts.

Let us always remember that spiritual gifts are given by God to equip people to serve the church and to bring glory to Him. We are not good singers, writers, preachers, teachers, or leaders because we are better than others, but because God has blessed us out of love. The gifts should bless the church, not stir up a spirit of jealousy or competition in the church.

God's Guidance

In addition to spiritual gifts, God gave us the Bible to serve as our manual in helping us to serve Him and guide us to heaven. The Lord enables us to understand the Word and apply it to our lives through the Holy Spirit's power. In *Christ's Object Lessons*, White tells us, "Without the Spirit of God a knowledge of His word is of no avail. The theory of truth, unaccompanied by the Holy Spirit, cannot quicken the soul or sanctify the heart. One may be familiar with the commands and promises of the Bible; but unless the Spirit of God sets the truth home, the character will not be transformed. Without the enlightenment of the Spirit, men will not be able to distinguish truth from error, and they will fall under the masterful temptations of Satan."[3] We can only understand the things of God through the grace of God.

Once we let the Lord into our lives, He makes it possible for us to serve Him; He guides our paths. Let us cooperate and listen to His voice. We will learn what He wants us to do. Indeed, it takes the grace of God for us to be still enough to learn from Him. But with total surrender, the Lord will ensure that we learn and grow, without which there would be a problem. Hebrew 5:12-14 says, "For though by this time you ought to be teachers, you need someone to teach you again the first principles of the oracles of God; and you have come to need milk and not solid food. For everyone who partakes only of milk is unskilled in the word of righteousness, for he is a babe. But solid food belongs to those who are of full age, that is, those who by reason of use have their senses exercised to discern both good and evil."

God designed sanctification for His people to keep growing until Jesus comes or until we rest while we await his second coming. Every Christian needs to keep growing. "But we all, with unveiled face, beholding as in a mirror the glory of the Lord, are being transformed into the same image from glory to glory, just as by the Spirit of the

Lord" (2 Corinthians 3:18). Yes, by beholding Christ, by reading the Word, contemplating upon it, by praying, we are changed from selfish, mean, rebellious people to God-fearing ones.

The Lord wants His people to remain connected to Him for life so that they may grow and lead others to the Savior. Jesus did not hesitate to tell us that without Him, we cannot do anything. God can make us fit for His work. All we need is to "lay it all at the altar," and allow Him to use us.

Our Experiences

Whether good or bad, our experiences make a significant contribution in preparing us to serve God and humankind. Previously, we saw that Moses had to be in the wilderness for 40 years, and Joseph became a slave in Egypt—experiences that prepared the two men for service. It is the same with us today. For instance, serving in a career, or going through a training course, equips us with knowledge in various fields. Better still, studying the Word of God leaves us wiser concerning matters of the gospel.

Moreover, enduring trials and temptations leaves us better fitted for services. God allows us to go through all these experiences for good reasons. In the end, we gain knowledge, learned skills, and wisdom to serve the church, and ultimately, to serve the Lord. Most times, we go through situations without us thinking that God is preparing us for service. Paul tells us, "in everything give thanks" (1Thessalonians 5:18).

During my undergraduate program, I took Christian Beliefs as one of the religious courses under general requirements. It was in that class where I first learned about the details of witnessing for God. I became very interested in testifying about the gospel, but I did not know how to do it. However, at college, I met a few lecturers who were real missionaries. Some of those men and women inspired me to teach in Christian schools, where I could encourage students to trust God and live for Him.

After I trained as a teacher, I became more determined to share Christ in schools where I taught and encouraged students and teachers to surrender to the Lord and to try Him in their lives. Thus, for many years, I had two deep-rooted desires: to write and to witness. For a long time, I sought to learn more about writing before I could embark on a writing project. But after a few months of learning, I was impressed to write without much delay. Then I started with a keen interest. An experience that did not mean much to me before turned out to be something I sincerely wanted to share with other people.

By the time I finished writing down all the stories I was impressed to write, I had a 146-page book about God's love, faithfulness, and power to save and to sustain His people. That was my first book: *God Makes a Way*. Looking back, I realize that it was not only in writing that God prepared me, but He also provided training for me before I served in every job that I did.

After I obtained a master's degree, I got a job at Century Park College in Kenya. My primary responsibility was to set up the education department for the college. As a result, I needed to facilitate and ensure that there was a relevant curriculum for each course in my department, sit in the interview panel to hire teachers, advertise for students and organize seminars to train teachers in charge of Guidance and Counseling in high schools. This job was very demanding, but I learned a lot from it.

Two years later, I got a job as the deputy principal of the Kitui Adventist School in Kenya, which comprised of a preschool, primary (elementary), and a high school. At one point, we had more than 700 students—400 boarders and 300 day scholars. Six months later, I became the principal of the school. The organization and leadership skills that I had learned at Century Park College became very handy. Even though I delegated many duties as the principal, I was still responsible for the effective implementation of the curriculum, maintaining discipline, and I was also the link between the school and the stakeholders. At Century Park, I learned a bit of each of those roles as a department head in a new college.

A few years later, I came to America to teach students with disabilities and behavioral challenges. The skills I learned as an administrator in previous schools prepared me to teach, guide students at my new job, and to communicate with parents. In each of the schools, I got a chance to witness for Christ to encourage others to give their lives to God. I learned that God trains His workers. Each job that I took prepared me for the next appointment. Over and over again, I have learned the need to surrender to God and to let Him lead me in every duty that He gives me.

Please, join me in prayer and ask God to teach and train us for ministry. All we need to do is to allow Him into our lives. He will lead each one of us through the right path, according to His will. And He will work through our ministries and make them successful for His glory.

Chapter 16

Your Service to God

While some people have identified ministries through which to serve God, others are yet to determine theirs. I am sure if we were all to share our experiences, we would hear different stories about serving. For many years, I heard fellow Christians talk about ministry, but I did not quite understand what they meant. Then I attended a function that my church organized to help people identify ministries through which they could serve. The organizers set up a big room with tables, each representing one of the church departments, such as those for women, men, children, prison, education, and the homeless.

There were more than 40 ministries in the church, and members were encouraged to join at least one, depending on their interests and knowledge. After going around the tables discussing different ministries and taking time to study the Bible, I learned that "there are diversities of gifts, but the same Spirit. There are differences of ministries, but the same Lord. And there are diversities of activities, but it is the same God who works all in all. But the manifestation of the Spirit is given to each one for the profit of all" (1 Corinthians 12:4–7). As the following verses tell us, the gifts are given,

> for the equipping of the saints for the work of ministry, for the edifying of the body of Christ, till we all come to the unity of the faith and of the knowledge of the Son of God, to a perfect man, to the measure of the stature of the fullness of Christ; that we should no longer be children, tossed to and fro and carried about

> with every wind of doctrine, by the trickery of men, in the cunning craftiness of deceitful plotting, but, speaking the truth in love, may grow up in all things into Him who is the head—Christ— from whom the whole body, joined and knit together by what every joint supplies, according to the effective working by which every part does its share, causes growth of the body for the edifying of itself in love. (Ephesians 4:12–16)

The gifts are given by God to each Christian to use in His service. Since we receive different gifts, we have various ministries ministering to the church to God's glory. The ministries are there to point people to God and to help them to grow spiritually. Even though the church encourages people to identify their gifts and use them, there are many times when the church recognizes talents in people and chooses them to serve in various departments.

The church then provides training to equip the people more for service. From experience in my walk with the Lord, I have come to believe that God is in charge of His work, and He provides leadership to all who will let Him. Over the years, I have found much joy in teaching. When I meet my former students, who are doing well in serving God and society, I thank God for His grace. Before I understood what ministry was all about, I did not realize that teaching was one of my gifts. All I knew was that I liked doing it, whether in church or school. I also realized that God had been leading me in ministries, even though I did not know it.

The Role of the Holy Spirit in our Ministries

Once we are filled with the Holy Spirit, He produces the fruit of the Spirit in us, without which we serve our selfish desires rather than God. For example, without love and longsuffering, we cannot reach out to prisoners and the homeless and show them the love of God. In *Counsels for Churches,* White says, "It is the absence of the

Spirit that makes the gospel ministry so powerless. Learning, talent, eloquence, every natural or acquired endowment, may be possessed; but, without the presence of the Spirit of God, no heart will be touched, no sinner won to Christ. On the other hand, if they are connected with Christ, if the gifts of the Spirit are theirs, the poorest and most ignorant of His disciples will have a power that will tell upon hearts. God makes them channels for the outflowing of the highest influence in the universe."[1] Every person who wants to succeed in serving God, regardless of the ministry, should pray daily for the Holy Spirit to fill the heart and to lead in the work. It is the Holy Spirit who enables us to serve the Lord, according to His will.

The Word of God and Your Ministry

Regardless of your ministry, the goal should be to lead others to Christ to be saved. Jesus commissioned his followers, "Go therefore and make disciples of all the nations, baptizing them in the name of the Father and of the Son and of the Holy Spirit, teaching them to observe all things that I have commanded you; and lo, I am with you always, even to the end of the age" (Matthew 28:19, 20). We are all called to participate in the work of pointing others to Christ to be saved. The specific way in which each of us accomplishes the mission depends on our spiritual gifts.

The world needs to know the love of God for each person, and each person needs to realize the necessity to decide to surrender oneself to Jesus willingly. Thus, even though there are many ways of reaching others for God, every Christian needs to understand the Word of God deeply and share it with others. Regardless of your ministry, the Bible should provide you with the principles that you will follow in your ministry.

What Is Your Ministry?

As stated earlier, ministries are created or chosen depending on spiritual gifts that God has bestowed on His people. To minimize frustrations in our service to God, we need to pray and ask the Lord to lead us to ministries where He wants us to serve. Graciously, God gives us different gifts, talents, personalities, and opportunities in various fields to have people work in all those areas. You may feel like you do not know "enough" to do the work. But Jesus knows everything, and as long as you have Him with you, He will continue to teach and guide you to serve Him.

The work of teaching, baptizing, and exhorting involves complementary activities in the church. No one can do everything alone. No one function can meet the diverse needs of the church by itself, so we need different gifts, skills, and personality traits. We learn from the apostle Paul, who said, "I planted, Apollos watered, but God gave the increase. So then neither he who plants is anything, nor he who waters, but God who gives the increase. Now he who plants and he who waters are one, and each one will receive his own reward according to his own labor. For we are God's fellow workers; you are God's field, you are God's building" (1 Corinthians 3:6–9). God works through those who are willing to be of service to Him. As we prayerfully study the Word daily, let us follow the leading of the Holy Spirit in serving God. Will you, prayerfully, identify your gift and serve the Lord?

Chapter 17

The Lord's Battle

Every time I read about God fighting our spiritual battles, a particular picture comes to mind. I imagine a situation where a father gets into a game with his child and another person. The child is too young to handle his or her opponent. So the father gets into the game to play on the side of the child. And when the father corners the child's opponent, the child gets the opportunity to kick the ball into the net and score. Then the child celebrates the victory together with the father. These facts never cease to impress me about the fathomless wisdom and love of God. I find it very encouraging that, as Christians, our primary role is to allow Christ to live in us and to let Him do His work through us. When that happens, others see the goodness of the Lord through us. Mathew 5:14 calls us to be "the light of the world, a city on a hill" that cannot be hidden.

However, God does not want us to worry about how or when people will get converted. Our part is to do the witnessing, teaching, and anything else, the Lord leads us to do for Him. If, when you teach, preach, or witness to people, they do not seem to be in a hurry to give themselves to the Lord, do not get discouraged. Let me tell you the story of my grandfather.

Winning Others Through Surrender

My paternal grandfather lived for more than 100 years, and until a few days before he passed away, he was not a Christian. Nobody expected him to get converted to the faith because he had never shown interest in Christianity. All his life, he had never paid attention to anybody talking about salvation. My grandfather was very strong-willed and aggressive. People feared him because he turned violent quickly. As time passed, he became old and weak. All he did was lie down in his bed. Nonetheless, his memory was good, and he talked clearly.

One day he fell sick. Then my parents took him to the hospital, where he ended up being hospitalized but refused to take medication. Whenever nurses gave medicine to him, he told them, "You are wasting time treating me. You cannot cure old age." After a few days in the hospital, he said to my father, "Take me back home. I want to die at home." My father was hesitant. But Grandpa insisted until my father gave in.

On staying home for about two days, Grandpa realized that he was not dying as soon as he expected. Then one morning, he called my mother and told her, "Ma Musya, (Musya's granddaughter), I want to talk to you." Traditionally, the Kamba people of Kenya call their daughters-in-law by the names of the women's paternal grandfathers. That is how a father or mother-in-law shows respect to their son's wife. My mother's grandfather was Musya; hence that is the name by which Grandpa addressed her. On that particular day, he called her and said, "Please, take a look in the middle of my head; there is something in there that prevents me from dying. Pull it out so that I can go to rest." My mother looked, but all she saw was a smooth scalp and grey hair.

"I don't see anything, Father," Mother told him.

"Okay, call Kilundo for me," he told her. Mother left to get my father, who came immediately. Then Grandpa started, "There is a man who teaches people about the God of heaven. The man lives in Ngosini village. Do you know him?" inquired Grandpa.

"Yes," said Father.

"Please go and tell him that I want to accept the God of Christians. Tell him to come and pray for me." Grandpa instructed Father.

The man that Grandpa was referring to was known as Aaron. He had migrated from Mbooni, one of the first places where Christianity was established in Ukambani, Kenya. Aaron gave his life to Christ and moved to another district, Makueni, to pursue more land for farming, just like my father and many other people did.

My parents could not believe what they heard Grandpa say. Both Mother and Father were Christians. All members of my family attended church. And even though Father rejected western education, he learned to read the Bible in Kikamba. He refused to visit witch doctors or to offer sacrifices to other gods. With the little light that he had, he rejected ancestral practices. One day Father told us, "Demon possession tortured my mother for many years. Many times, she would get up and run to the woods at night. She would scream and run through thorny bushes throughout the night. I don't want anything to do with Satan."

Now that Grandpa wanted to give his life to God, my father was overjoyed. He gladly went for Aaron. About an hour later, Father and Aaron arrived at Grandpa's hut. "I want to give my life to the God of Christians," said Grandpa. Aaron prayed for him and led him to pledge his commitment to God. A day later, Grandpa died. The whole village marveled at that turn of events in his life. Nobody imagined that he would ever give a chance to God. People were surprised because Grandpa had lived in Mbooni and had seen the missionaries and what they did for many years before he migrated to Makueni. But he had rejected Christianity and anything to do with it. People did not know that, from a distance, he had accumulated knowledge about Christianity and the "God of Christians."

Grandpa knew that, one day, God will resurrect Christians, and they will live forever, never to grow old or to die again. Throughout his life, he was active and hardworking. But life became very frustrating to him when he became too old to get out of bed or to slaughter his cows for meat, which he loved doing. His gods had failed him because they had promised him life and protection. After Mother was unable to see the "thing" on his head, he told her that a witch doctor had put something in his head, promising him that he would never die as long as he had that object in his head. All this turned out to be a lie because when the time came for him to die, he died.

Both Grandpa and Grandma lived on my parents' farm, a little distance away from our homestead. My siblings and I visited our grandparents daily. Every mealtime Mother gave us food to take to our grandparents before we sat down to eat. And I can still remember Grandpa's superstitious practices that proved to be of no help to him by the time he surrendered his life to God.

Later, when I became a mature Christian, I learned a great lesson from my grandfather's life story. I realized that despite his superstitious practices, Christian teachings, and the exemplary lives of Christians around him made an impact on him without people knowing. I got encouraged that the Holy Spirit works in marvelous ways.

As a Christian who is interested in witnessing for God, I learned that I need to tell people about the saving grace of the Lord. It is even more important to live my life as a surrendered Christian. Whether people give their lives to Jesus immediately or not, that should not discourage me. My task is to spread the Word. The Holy Spirit will convert hearts in His own way in His own time. My grandfather's story encourages me not to give up on anyone.

Even though God does not call all of us to be pastors, we are all called to point others to Christ. Like the Samaritan woman, let us all witness. Every person who has encountered the Savior has a story to tell others about the Lord. Even when we are not formally teaching people the Word of God, our lives should continually do the work of witnessing, and the Lord will bless our efforts with much fruit to His glory. White tells us,

> There is no limit to the usefulness of one who, by putting self aside, makes room for the working of the Holy Spirit upon his heart, and lives a life wholly consecrated to God. If men will endure the necessary discipline, without complaining, or fainting, by the way, God will teach them hour by hour, and day by day. He longs to reveal His grace. If His people will remove the obstructions, He will pour forth the waters of salvation in abundant streams through the human channels.[1]

The life of a sincere Christian is a strong sermon to the world. The endurance that we need to do God's work requires total surrender. Let us surrender to the Lord so that He may give us the grace to serve Him, according to His will.

Chapter 18

Victory Is Assured

The *Oxford Living Dictionaries* define victory as "an act of defeating an enemy or opponent in a battle, game, or other competition."[1] But The *King James Bible Dictionary* gives the exact meaning of victory as is used in this chapter. It defines it as a "defeat of an enemy in battle" and also as "the advantages or superiority gained over spiritual enemies, over passions and appetites, or over temptations, or in any struggle."[2] Thus, if there is victory, there must be an opponent or obstacle that the victor must overcome to triumph. And while there are various settings where people strive to become winners, such as in games, competitions, or wars, I will use the pursuit of university degrees as an example of how people endeavor to overcome obstacles to achieve much-desired rewards or victory. This scenario fascinates me because every time I pursue a course at a university, I obtain a list of all the requirements that I must fulfill to receive my certificate.

Then as I go through the course, I put a checkmark against every class that I complete successfully. Once I meet all the requirements, I know it is time to graduate from the program. Now think about the triumph involving our lives. I am talking about our victory to receive eternal life. The death of Jesus Christ met all the requirements for our salvation. The plan is complete. God sent His Son to this world to mingle with humans, to teach them, and to die for them so that whoever believes in Him will receive eternal life. I find many similarities between the plan of salvation and the conquest of the city of Jericho. Look at the way the Israelites gained their victory over the people and the city of Jericho:

> And it came to pass, when Joshua was by Jericho, that he lifted his eyes and looked, and behold, a Man stood opposite him with His sword drawn in His hand. And Joshua went to Him and said to Him, "Are You for us or for our adversaries?"
>
> So He said, "No, but as Commander of the army of the LORD I have now come."
>
> And Joshua fell on his face to the earth and worshiped, and said to Him, "What does my Lord say to His servant?"
>
> Then the Commander of the LORD's army said to Joshua, "Take your sandal off your foot, for the place where you stand is holy." And Joshua did so. ((Joshua 5:13–15)

The episode described in the preceding verses gives us a perfect example of victory for God's people through God's hand. Joshua was about to lead the Israelites to take Jericho. Then the Man with a drawn sword appeared. Joshua wanted to know whether the Man was coming in support of or against Israel. "No, but as Commander of the army of the Lord I have now come," said the Man who seems to have been Christ Himself. An angel would not have accepted Joshua's worship. The Commander of the Lord's army came in-person to lead the Israelites to take Jericho.

Then Joshua, realizing that he was standing in front of the Lord, demonstrated humility and surrender to the Lord. Scripture tells us that Joshua fell on his face and worshipped. He asked, "What does my Lord say to His servant?" Joshua surrendered to the Lord and asked for instructions, which he followed accordingly.

Then the Lord conquered Jericho on behalf of the Israelites. All the people of God had to do was to march around the city of Jericho seven times. The walls collapsed, giving victory to the Israelites. To me, this is one of the most encouraging stories in the Bible. I like the fact that when Joshua was bracing himself to lead the Israelites to take the city of Jericho, Jesus was already there to fight the battle Himself. Remember, Joshua was one of the 12 men who spied Canaan, way before Moses died. And Joshua and Caleb were the only two spies, out of 12, who had faith that God was able to take the land of Canaan for His people despite its strong inhabitants and strongly fortified cities.

According to Joshua and Caleb, nothing could thwart God from fulfilling His promise to Abraham's descendants. Joshua's belief that God was going to take the land of Canaan for His people would be the only sensible reason for him to lead the Israelites even to attempt to attack such a city as Jericho. And look at God's faithfulness. He kept His promise to His people. That shows that we can always trust God's promise that He will never abandon us or fail to keep any of His promises to us.

The most exciting promise of all is our eternal life in paradise, for which Jesus paid the price. All we have to do is accept God's offer by faith and allow Him to lead us to heaven. Before then, we must be conscious of the battle that is going on between good and evil. In the same way the Israelites could not take the land of Canaan by their strength, we too are unable to win the battle between good and evil. Hence, the Lord wants us to surrender to Him and allow Him to fight for us.

Let me give you another example of our spiritual battle in this life. We face a similar situation like the one described in 2 Chronicles 20, in which the people of Judah learned that a multitude from Moab, Ammon, and those of Mount Seir had united against them. Judah, together with their king, Jehoshaphat, got terribly afraid. They knew that on their own, they had no strength to defeat the multitude. Then Jehoshaphat called all the people of Judah together to cry to the Lord for help. Judah fasted and prayed, and through Jahaziel, the Lord told them, “Listen, all you of Judah and you inhabitants of Jerusalem, and you, King Jehoshaphat! Thus says the LORD to you: ‘Do not be afraid nor dismayed because of this great multitude, for the battle is not yours, but God's’” (verse 15). God promised to fight for them. And He did. The Israelites defeated their enemies without raising a spear. The multitudes fought one another and killed themselves. God has the same power and love for His people today. All that we need for our salvation was finished at the cross by our Savior, Jesus Christ. Our victory for our daily battles is assured. Our eternal salvation is assured. “It is finished,” Jesus said.

Power to Overcome

Sin does not have to hinder anyone from entering heaven. If we sin, and confess our sins and repent, God does not only forgive us but also cleanses us “from all unrighteousness” (1John 1:9). Additionally, Christ died to destroy the power of sin, and now He is our advocate—one who prays for us and intercedes on our behalf. The following verse attests to this:

> If anyone sins, we have an Advocate with the Father, Jesus Christ the righteous. And He Himself is the propitiation for our sins, and not for ours only but also for the whole world. Now by this we know that we know Him, if we keep His commandments. He who says, “I know Him,” and does not keep His commandments is a liar, and the truth is not in him. But whoever keeps His word, truly the love of God is perfected in him. By this we know that we are in Him. He who says he abides in Him ought himself also to walk just as He walked. (1 John 2:1–6)

The secret of receiving victory over anything that draws us away from God is our relationship with the Savior and Lord, Jesus Christ. As long as we have a relationship with Him, we will learn from Him. We will receive power from Him. Our relationship with Him will demonstrate our love toward Him. Jesus says that if a person loves Him, he or she will keep His commandments. Of course, without a relationship with Him, we will not be able to obey Him.

Victory Through Faith

God created everything by His power. Whatever the Lord commanded through His Word came into being: He made the heavens, angels, sun, moon, stars, water—everything (Genesis 1:1, 3; Psalm 33:6). We, too, are His creation, and He saves us from our sins by His power, by grace. God creates us anew through the blood of His Son, Jesus Christ. He saves us from sinful life to holy living. The Lord can strengthen us to overcome every sin and every addiction. We just need to let Him work it out for us. "For whatever is born of God overcomes the world. And this is the victory that has overcome the world—our faith. Who is he who overcomes the world, but he who believes that Jesus is the Son of God?" (1 John 5:4, 5). Repeatedly, the Bible tells us that our salvation is a done deal. And we need to believe in the Lord and allow Him to enable us to cooperate with Him to receive eternal life.

God fights for us to overcome. He makes sure that we have the needed help to overcome temptations. He also provides the weapons with which to fight the spiritual war. The ammunition must come from Him because they "are not carnal; they are but mighty through God to the pulling down of strongholds; Casting down arguments, and every high thing that exalts itself against the knowledge of God, and bringing into captivity every thought to the obedience of Christ"

(2 Corinthians 10:4, 5). God's power overcomes the enemy and all the workings of evil.

When we allow God's power to prevail in our lives, miracles happen. Reading the Word, continually praying, and cooperating with the Holy Spirit releases the strength to resist evil in a Christian's life. Jude emphasizes the same truth that God is able to keep us from falling. Once people surrender themselves to Him, there is no obstacle that He cannot overcome for them. He enables us to triumph over every hindrance. In *The Great Controversy*, White says, "Neither wicked men nor devils can hinder the work of God, or shut out His presence from His people, if they will, with subdued, contrite hearts, confess and put away their sins, and in faith claim His promises. Every temptation, every opposing influence, whether open or secret, may be successfully resisted."[3]

Let us make use of the resources that God gives us for our help. "And they overcame him by the blood of the Lamb and by the word of their testimony, and they did not love their lives to the death" (Revelation 12:11). Yes, by the blood of the lamb, Jesus Christ, and by the word of our testimony, we will overcome the evil one. These are the resources for our victory. Thus, we need to set time to study the Bible and pray for God's Spirit to fill our hearts daily. We are free to claim our victory through the name of Jesus Christ. The discipline to spend meaningful time with God every day is in itself part of our success in our spiritual battle. May each one of us ask the Lord for strength to overcome.

Jesus lived on earth, so He very much understands what we go through. He was also tempted like us, yet He did not sin. God permits us to approach Him for help. Will you join me daily to pray for the grace to surrender ourselves to God to live a victorious life?

Chapter 19

Choice and Destiny

The choices we make in this life will determine our eternal destiny. God created us with the capacity to make decisions. Even though He does not want anyone to perish, He allows us to choose our destiny without coercion. Through the Scriptures and the Holy Spirit, we learn that if we allow Jesus to be our Savior and Lord, we are choosing everlasting life. But if we reject Him, we are choosing eternal death.

The importance of choosing good over evil, life over death, is emphasized throughout the Bible. Genesis 3 chronicles the life of Adam and Eve in the Garden of Eden, their decision to eat the forbidden fruit, and the consequences that followed. It was all a matter of choice. Later, just before the children of Israel entered the promised land, they were cautioned about the importance of making choices according to the Lord's guidance. Moses spoke to the people to understand the seriousness of their decisions and actions once they crossed the Jordan River into Canaan:

> See, I have set before you today life and good, death and evil, in that I command you today to love the LORD your God, to walk in His ways, and to keep His commandments, His statutes, and His judgments, that you may live and multiply; and the LORD your God will bless you in the land which you go to possess. But if your heart turns away so that you do not hear, and are drawn away, and worship other gods and serve them, I announce to you

today that you shall surely perish; you shall not prolong your days in the land which you cross over the Jordan to go in and possess. (Deuteronomy 30:15–18)

The children of Israel had to decide between worshipping the God of heaven, who delivered them from slavery or worshipping idols that the people of Canaan worshipped. Each of those choices had consequences. Talking about choices and consequences gives me flashbacks to my teenage and young adult years. There were seven children in my family—five girls and two boys. A week would hardly pass without either our mother or father talking to us about choices, whether it concerned working hard on the farm or studying diligently to develop a career. However, when we became teenagers, the importance of making the right decisions and the consequences that resulted from poor choices was discussed more frequently. At the time, the talk revolved more around choosing life partners and what to expect, depending on the kind of a husband or wife one chose.

My mother believed that one's life partner had a significant impact on one's life. To explain that to us, she had a favorite quote: "All the pieces of meat are on a plate. Each one of you should choose whichever piece you want. Whether you want to chew on a bone or to eat a steak is up to you." The bone and steak represented the quality of life each of us would expect, depending on the life partner one chose.

I believe that it is common knowledge that choices have consequences because we experience that reality all the time. For instance, if you desire to have oranges in your garden, you plant an orange tree. You cannot plant a mango tree and expect to harvest oranges. If a person wants to become a lawyer, a doctor, a teacher, or any other professional, one must pursue the relevant course of study. Our choices are a crucial part of our lives. One thing we should always remember is that our choices are not only limited to this life but determine our lives in the world to come.

Joshua told the Israelites, “Choose for yourselves this day whom you will serve, whether the gods which your fathers served that were on the other side of the River, or the gods of the Amorites, in whose land you dwell. But as for me and my house, we will serve the LORD” (Joshua 24:15). What a powerful statement to declare one's stand on such a matter of life and death!

It is equally crucial to recognize our dependency on God, without whose grace it is impossible to follow through with our desires or decisions to live for Him and to bring Him glory. No wonder the Lord tells us to trust in Him totally and not to depend on our strength or understanding. Every person needs to make a deliberate decision to surrender to the Lord, by God's grace, and remain on His side throughout one's life.

The eternal destiny of all human beings boils down to good and evil, life or death. The end for some people will be everlasting life with God, while for others, it will be eternal death. Neither God nor Satan will take anybody to any of these destinies by force. Our individual choices and the kind of life each one chooses to live in this life will determine where we will each spend eternity. Yes, our decisions and our actions on earth are important. “For we must all appear before the judgment seat of Christ, that each one may receive the things done in the body, according to what he has done, whether good or bad” (2 Corinthians 5:10). Our actions follow the decisions and choices that we make.

If we choose to allow Christ into our lives and to form a loving relationship with Him, that bond is reflected in our relationships with others, and it is all a matter of choice. Dr. Mathew Jennings states, “When we exercise the will and freely choose what is right, God imbues the mind with divine energy that provides the strength necessary to break free from destructive patterns of living. As apostle Paul said, we become '"partakers of the divine nature"' and live in harmony with God and His methods (2 Peter 1:4)."[1]

But if we allow Satan to take control of our minds, our actions will show. Again, all this is a matter of choice. When we choose Jesus and surrender to Him totally, He guides us. Then we do not need to worry about producing good deeds, for Christ ensures that it happens. Once Christ resides in our hearts, our thoughts, choices, and actions become aligned with Him. "But thanks be to God, who gives us the victory through our Lord Jesus Christ" (1 Corinthians 15:57). Our victory and eternal life depend on our choices.

John 3:16 is one of the Bible verses greatly recited by both children and adult Christians. And the clear, straight forward message in this verse is one of the choices and consequences. Out of love, God gave His Son, Jesus Christ, so that any person who believes in Him will be saved. So, those who trust Jesus enough to allow Him to be their Savior and Lord will get eternal life. Now, what is the opposite of the message in John 3:16? Simply, any person who will reject or who will not believe in Jesus Christ will not receive everlasting life. As simple and straightforward as this verse is, it is profound. It talks to us about the seriousness of our decision and the choice we make between God and Satan. There is no middle ground. If you choose God, you automatically reject Satan. The reverse is also true.

The Power of Choice

More than a decade ago, I attended a relative's funeral, and while I have forgotten most of the details, one thing remains fresh in my mind. Almost every speaker who belonged to the church that my relative attended before he died concluded his or her speech with this one sentence: "God keep him where he chose for himself when he was alive." Wow! I had never heard anybody say that so candidly at a funeral. The sentence sounded very strong at the time. Yet, it is the reality of the Word of God. While people are still alive, they choose their destiny for eternity. Even though the dead will wait in their graves until Jesus comes the second time, the truth remains that after death, people cannot change their minds. Whatever they chose when they were alive will affect them eternally. Even failure to choose is choosing. Pastor Randy Skeet said, "If you are not serving God wholly, you are serving the devil full time." Salvation is available for any person who believes in the Son of God. I am glad that no human being or even Satan has the power to prevent anyone from being saved if the person yields his or her heart to God. Faith in the Savior is powerful enough to overcome any obstacle.

Good and Evil

Since the inception of sin, when Satan chose to disobey God, there have been two forces in life—good and evil. The Bible clearly states what is good or right and what is evil. Whatever the Bible calls sin, is sin no matter how many people practice it. John 3:16 expounds distinctly on the consequences associated with either choice. The story of Adam and Eve is an excellent example of the relationship between choice and destiny. God made it plain to Adam and Eve that they had a decision to make. If they did not eat the fruit from the Tree of Knowledge of Good and Evil, they would live forever. But if they ate fruit from the forbidden tree, they would surely die. Adam and Eve chose to disobey God. Instead of living forever, a time came when they died as a result of their decision to disobey God. We face a similar decision today. The Word of God still stands. Disobedience to the revealed will of God, as we see it in the Bible, is sin.

A lawyer confronted Jesus with a question about what he needed to do to get salvation. Even though the lawyer was looking for a way to trap Jesus, the Lord's answer to the question is valid for us to use in answering the same question today. The lawyer asked, "Teacher, what shall I do to inherit eternal life?" (Luke 10:25). In response, Jesus affirmed the Word of God: "You shall love the Lord your God with all your heart, with all your soul, with all your strength, and with all your mind, and your neighbor as yourself" (verses 27, 28). Jesus' response gives us a summary of what will happen if we surrender to Him. When we choose to give our lives to God, instead of to the enemy, God provides us with the grace to love Him with all our hearts, souls, strength, and our minds. God is so merciful and gracious.

Can you imagine spending eternity with someone whom you do not love? That would be the worst punishment in the universe. God makes sure that this will not happen by enabling us to love Him more than anything else or anybody else. Surely, heaven will be a place of joy for those who accept Jesus Christ to be the Savior and Lord of their lives. Those who choose to go to heaven need to love others as themselves. God makes it possible for this to happen for those who surrender their lives to Him.

God is love, and He teaches His children to love. Once we learn to love God, we get the grace to love others as we love ourselves. Remember, God does not leave us to figure out what it means to love Him with all our hearts, souls, strength, and minds. He gives us details on how to do that. The first four commandments in Exodus 20:1–11 guide us on how to love and obey God. The last six commandments teach us how to love our fellow human beings. The principles expressed in the Ten Commandments run throughout the Bible. No wonder Jesus said that on the two commandments hang all the law and the prophets. Can you imagine everything we need to inherit eternal life is provided to us? All we need to do is to accept it.

Just like Adam and Eve, we all have free will to choose God or to reject Him. Since the rebellion of Satan, the devil became the rival of God. Satan wants people to choose him over God. Yes, the devil wants people to worship him even though worship belongs to God alone. He was even shameless enough to tell Jesus to worship him in the wilderness. Nonetheless, God encourages all people to choose Him and to take Jesus Christ as their Savior and Lord of their lives, so that they may receive eternal life.

Living According to Our Choices

After we make up our minds to accept God in our lives, Scripture tells us, "I say then: Walk in the Spirit, and you shall not fulfill the lust of the flesh. For the flesh lusts against the Spirit, and the Spirit against the flesh; and these are contrary to one another, so that you do not do the things that you wish" (Galatians 5:16, 17). We can only walk in the Spirit if we allow the Spirit to dwell in our hearts.

We need to understand that what we will face at the end of life on earth depends on the path we take in this life. Our only opportunity to pick a side is now; we will have no control over our destiny after we die. God "will render to each one according to his deeds: eternal life to those who by patient continuance in doing good seek for glory, honor, and immortality; but those who are self-seeking and do not obey the truth, but obey unrighteousness—indignation and wrath" (Romans 2:6–8). To add to that plain statement, the Word of God tells us, "Depart from evil, and do good; And dwell forevermore" (Psalm 37:27). God calls on everybody to turn away from sin, for it leads to death. Let me explain this with a story.

A Cobra in a Gourd

A story is told about a man and his wife, who lived in Machakos, Kenya. The couple kept a beautiful gourd in which they kept *ikii*, a unique traditional porridge. Every day the man took his cattle out to pasture and to the river to drink water. He would return home around midday, take the gourd and a half calabash (*nzele*), sit under a tree shade, and pour cold porridge in the half calabash to drink. Both the man and his wife would enjoy the special porridge to quench their thirst after working in the hot sun, but for the man, it was a special ritual that he never skipped.

Whenever porridge was finished in the gourd, they cleaned it before pouring in fresh porridge. One day, after drinking their porridge, they cleaned the gourd and put it outside the house to dry in the sunshine. The man took his cattle to graze as usual while the wife went to the river to fetch water. Later, when they returned home, the gourd was dry and ready for fresh porridge to be poured in. They poured fresh, cold *ikii* in the gourd and kept it until the next day when they would enjoy their delicacy.

The following day, the man came home and went straight for the gourd and a half calabash, ready to quench his thirst with *ikii*. However, when he opened the gourd lid, he saw a cobra staring back at him. He realized that when the gourd was left outside the house to dry, a snake had entered the clean, warm gourd. But they did not notice when they poured their porridge the previous day. *How could he get the snake out without breaking their precious gourd?* He wondered.

With a long stick, the man tried to roll the gourd on the ground, but the snake stayed put. For hours he turned, pushed, and shook the gourd in vain. As the evening approached, the man became more concerned about the poisonous snake. He did not want to give the snake a chance to slither out at night and bite them. Later, his wife joined him, and their last option was to burn the gourd to get rid of the cobra. Despite the couple's love for their gourd, they sadly pushed it outside the homestead and burned it together with the snake.

The everlasting fire is prepared for the devil and his angels (Matthew 25:41). God desires that all humankind be saved. That is why He gave His son to die for everybody. Sin is hideous and deadly. It will be quite unfortunate if a person harbors it in his or her life because the person will get destroyed together with the sin. This may sound harsh, but it is the truth that God will destroy sin and get rid of it forever, no matter where it will be hidden (Mathew 13:47-50).

We have a golden opportunity now to receive Jesus as our Savior and Lord of our lives, and He will cleanse us from all our sins. He will empower us to overcome sin. Let us allow the Lord in our lives now. He will prepare us for his kingdom through faith in Jesus Christ.

Chapter 20

Getting Ready for the Kingdom

I trust that you want to spend eternity with God. I, too, want to be there. Personally, the main reason why I want to go to heaven is to spend my life with a God whose love, kindness and goodness are unfathomable. There is not enough room in this book to list all the verses that talk about God's goodness. Have you ever spent time with a loving, generous, courteous, graceful, and intelligent person? I mean somebody who's presence emits love and serenity. I know there are not many such people on earth, but I was blessed to have a few in my life. One of them was my father. But my father was not perfect; only God is. I try to imagine how it will feel, what it will be like, to be in God's presence.

I want to go to heaven, sit at the feet of Jesus, and watch His face in a place where there will be no pain, mourning, or dying (Isaiah 25:8; Revelation 21:4). Can you imagine living in a paradise where every need you have is satisfied? Yes, a home where you will genuinely love everyone and where everyone will love you deeply. I once read a book whose main character talked about loving somebody "idiotically madly." I do not remember the analysis of that kind of love, but I know that the love we will experience in heaven will be "the real stuff."

If you have not yet received Jesus Christ as your Savior, I pray that you do it now so that your life will be secure in God's hands. Please pray this prayer:

Father God of heaven, I surrender my life to You. I take Jesus Christ to be my Savior and the Lord of my life. Please, forgive all my sins and give me the power to overcome all evil. Fill me with Your Holy Spirit. Give me the grace to study Your Word daily and enable me to understand it and to follow. I pray that Your will be done in my life. I pray in the name of Jesus Christ, my Savior, and Lord. Amen.

After you accept Jesus as your Savior and the Lord of your life, please, continue to study the Bible. The Word of God teaches us about God and guides us on how to live our lives to His glory. Keep company with mature Christians and join a church that is genuinely rooted in the Word of God. Mature Christians will give you the support you need to grow spiritually. Pray and ask God to lead you in this process.

All on the Altar

For those of us who identify ourselves as Christians, God's Word tells us, "Examine yourselves as to whether you are in the faith. Test yourselves" (2 Corinthians 13:5). A true Christian—one who has given oneself totally to God—is known by the manifestation of the Holy Spirit in the life of the person. The fruit of the Holy Spirit is seen in the life of the person. I like the fact that Scripture tells us to examine and to test ourselves to know whether we are in the faith. Is my life in total alignment with the Word of God? Am I at peace with my conscience, or does it nag me about a sin in my life? This is a question that all serious Christians should ask themselves. I am talking about giving oneself totally to God, a hundred percent. Let me explain this with the following testimony.

On February 15, 2018, I joined a group of other believers on a mission trip, organized by Maranatha Volunteers International, to Kenya. Like everybody else in the group, I was looking forward to serving and blessing the community we were visiting. I chose to teach children through the Vacation Bible Study (VBS) program, and I was excited to share the Word of God with the children and their teachers. But in the process, two things happened.

First, I learned that God had a specific work for me to do on the mission trip. Out of the 51 people who went on the trip, I was the only one who understood and spoke Swahili. The VBS group went to five different schools, and in the first school, we realized that there was a need for a translator. Most of the young children did not understand English, and even the older ones who understood English experienced difficulty understanding the American accent. Hence, the VBS group asked me to be the first to talk to the gatherings of children and teachers in Swahili and explain to them the process of the program and what we needed them to do. By God's grace, everything went well as we covered the five schools.

In one of the schools, we built a dining hall and a kitchen, which was the main project for the mission trip. In that school, there were many poor children, including orphans. I got a chance to speak to the whole congregation to encourage them with my experience as someone who grew up in a low-income family in Kenya. I told them that giving my life to God at an early age established a relationship with the Lord, which blessed me in many ways. For example, it saw me through school and career development until I later came to America as a missionary teacher. I was glad that they felt blessed by the testimony. But the best part was yet to come.

The second thing that happened was that in the process of leading the VBS program, the children preached to me through a Swahili song in a way that no sermon had done for many years. They sang, "Wakristo simama, simama imara, msiwe kama popo sidege, msiwe kama popo sidege simnyama," meaning Christians stand firm in your faith. Do not be like the bat, which is neither a bird nor an animal. Of course, we know that bats are mammals, but they have some of the characteristics of birds. So for a few seconds, I pictured a bat in my mind and realized that it has wings, and it flies; yet it is not a bird. It is a mammal—the only mammal that truly soars. Thus, even though bats have that major bird characteristic of flying, they are genuinely mammals, and feed their young ones with milk.

Then the children's message sank in. Some Christians are neither fully on the side of God, nor are they entirely in the world. They have some characteristics that other Christians have, but they also have a lot of worldly practices in their lives, such as cherished sins. They go to church, but they do not surrender themselves wholly to God. They do not allow the power of God to change them and empower them to overcome sin. Ellen White had much to say about this situation. In the book *Counsels for the Church,* she states,

> Today a large part of those who compose our congregations are dead in trespasses and sins. They come and go like the door upon its hinges. For years they have complacently listened to the most solemn, soul-stirring truths, but they have not put them in practice. Therefore they are less and less sensible of the preciousness of truth. The stirring testimonies of reproof and warning do not arouse them to repentance... While making a profession, they deny the power of godliness. If they continue in this state, God will reject them. They are unfitting themselves to be members of His family.[1]

So, the children's message through the Swahili song was timely. Christians need to firmly stand on the side of God but not be like the bat.

When we got back to Texas, I was one of the people who spoke at our church to report on the mission trip. I told the church members that while God gave me the burden of sharing His Word with the Turkana children, He spoke to me through a simple Swahili song, which they sang. The message I passed on to my church is the same message I am emphasizing here: Stand firm for Jesus. God calls us to surrender to Him. He calls us to establish a healthy, loving relationship with Him, which will give us the power to overcome every evil.

It is a waste of time to be a half-hearted, lukewarm Christian because God wants the whole of us or nothing. To the half-surrendered, Christ says, "I know your works, that you are neither cold nor hot. I could wish you were cold or hot" (Revelation, 3:15). While God desires that every person will be saved, He is honest with us. He tells us that surrendering just a part of us to Him while living the other part in sin will not help us because sin will not enter heaven. But to those who choose to give their lives totally to Him, He promises: "I will come again and receive you to Myself; that where I am, there you may be also" (John 14:3). "And God will wipe away every tear from their eyes; there shall be no more death, nor sorrow, nor crying" (Revelation 21:4). When I read these verses about what God has prepared for those who love Him, I am ready to surrender anything for heaven. God wants all of us there.

Let us surrender ourselves totally to the Lord and allow Him to change us to be like Him. Then He will take us to heaven when He comes again. May God lead us in every step of our lives until we meet in heaven.

ENDNOTES

Chapter 1

1. Ellen G. White, *Ministry of Healing,* 514, accessed June 4, 2018, https://m.egwwritings.org/en/book/135.2712#2712.
2. History.com, "Nelson Mandela Released From Prison," accessed June 4, 2018, www.history.com/this-day-in-history/nelson-mandelareleased-from-prison.

Chapter 2

1. Quote by C. S. Lewis, *Mere Christianity*, accessed May 6, 2018, www.goodreads.com/quotes/325809-for-pride-is-spiritual-cancer-it-eats-up-the-very.
2. *King James Bible Dictionary*: "self-sufficiency," accessed November 1, 2019, http://kingjamesbibledictionary.com/Dictionary/self-sufficiency.
3. Ellen G. White, *The Desire of Ages*, 300, accessed June 4, 2018, https://m.egwwritings.org/en/book/39.1823.
4. The *Cambridge English Dictionary*, "arrogance," accessed October 20, 2019, https://dictionary.cambridge.org/us/dictionary/english/arrogance.
5. Lewis, *Mere Christianity,* accessed May 6, 2018, https://www.goodreads.com/quotes/56967-as-long-as-you-are-proud-you-cannot-know-god.
6. John Dickson, *Humilitas*: *A Lost Key to Life, Love, and Leadership* (Grand Rapids, MI: Zondervan, 2011), 24.137.

Chapter 3

1. The *King James Version Bible Dictionary*, "unbelief," accessed December 30, 2019, www.av1611.com/kjbp/kjv dictionary/unbelief.html.
2. Ellen G. White, *The Great Controversy,* 527, accessed December 30, 2019, https://www.ellenwhite.info/books/ellen-g-white-book great-controversy-GC-32.htm.
3. White, *Testimonies for the Church*, Vol. 5, 675–676, accessed December 30, 2019, www.m.egwwritings.org/en/book/113.3270#3270.
4. Timothy R. Jennings, *Could It Be This Simple? A Biblical Model For Healing The Mind* (Chattanooga, TN: Lennox Publishing,2012), 133.

Chapter 4

1. *Cambridge Dictionary*, "fear," accessed October 15, 2018. www.dictionary.cambridge.org/us/dictionary/english/fear.
2. Ellen G. White, *Steps to Christ* (Nampa, ID: Pacific Press Publishing Association, 2000), 91.
3. White, *Steps to Christ,* 74.

Chapter 5

1. Jennings, *Could It Be This Simple? A Biblical Model For Healing The Mind,* 104.
2. *Seventh-day Bible Commentary* on the Book of John, (Hagerstown, MD: Review and Herald Publishing Association, 1980), 5:1036.

Chapter 6

1. Ellen G. White, *Steps to Christ,* 22.138.

Chapter 7

1. *Seventh-day Bible Commentary* on the Book of Genesis, (Hagerstown, MD: Review and Herald Publishing Association, 1978), 1:463.

Chapter 8

1. Ellen G. White, *Steps to Christ,* 30.
2. William Hendriksen, *New Testament Commentary: Romans* (Grand Rapids, MI: Baker Book, 1981), 406.
3. White, *The Desire of Ages,* 251.

Chapter 9

1. *Lexico Dictionary*, "peculiar," accessed September 20, 2019, www.lexico.com/definition/peculiar.
2. *Seventh-day Bible Commentary* on the book of Titus (Hagerstown, MD: Review and Herald Publishing Association, 1978), 7:367.
3. Ellen G. White, *Education*, 260, accessed July 18, 2018, www.whiteestate.org/books/ed/ed30.html.
4. White, *The Desire of Ages,* 668.

Chapter 10

1. Timothy R. Jennings, *Could It Be This Simple? A Biblical Model For Healing The Mind*, 104.
2. White, *The Desire of Ages,* 668.
3. Jennings, *Could It Be This Simple? A Biblical Model For Healing The Mind,* 99.

Chapter 11

1. Ellen G. White, *The Bible Echo*, September 24, 1894, para. 2, www.m.egwwritings.org/en/book/459.660 (accessed May 5, 2018).139.

Chapter 12

1. Ellen G. White, *Counsels on Health*, 367, accessed May 5, 2018).www.m.egwwritings.org/en/book/20.1906#1906.
2. White, *The Desire of Ages,* 331.

Chapter 13

1. Ellen G. White, *The Desire of Ages,* 417.
2. White, *Ministry of Healing,* 480.

Chapter 14

1. Ellen G. White, *The Desire of Ages,* 151–152.

Chapter 15

1. Ibid., 251.
2. White, *Ministries of Healing,* 513.
3. White, *Christ's Object Lessons*, 408, accessed June 4, 2018, https://m.egwwritings.org/en/book/15.1833.

Chapter 16

1. Ellen G. White, *Counsels for Churches* (Nampa, ID: Pacific Press Publishing Association, 1991), 100.

Chapter 17

1. Ellen G. White, *On Various Topics*, 7, accessed June 4, 2018, 140 www.shepherds-rod.org/dsdaboard/docs/surrend.htm.

Chapter 18

1. *The Oxford Living Dictionary*, "victory," accessed July 26, 2018, www.en.oxforddictionaries.com/definition/victory.
2. *King James Bible Dictionary*, "Victory," accessed November 2, 2018, www.kingjamesbibledictionary.com/Dictionary/victory.

3. Ellen G. White, *The Great Controversy,* 529, accessed July 26, 2018, www.ellenwhite.info/books/ellen-g-white-book-greatcontroversy-gc-32.htm .

Chapter 19

1. Jennings, *Could It Be This Simple? A Biblical Model For Healing The Mind*, 133.

Chapter 20

1. Ellen G. White, *Counsels for the Church*, 67.

Made in USA - Kendallville, IN
1218467_9780578670171
02.22.2021 1608